Publishing and Selling Your Book

MADE EASY

McDougal & Associates

Servants of Christ and Stewards of the Mysteries of God

Publishing and Selling Your Book

MADE EASY

by

Harold McDougal

References marked "KJV" are from the authorized King James Version of the Bible. References marked "NLT" are from *The New Living Translation of the Bible*, copyright © 1996 by Tyndale House Publishers, Inc., Wheaton, Illinois. References marked "AMP" are from *The Amplified Bible*, copyright © 1954, 1958, 1962, 1964, 1965, 1987 by The Lockman Foundation, La Habra, California. References marked "NKJV" are from the *Holy Bible, New King James Version,* copyright © 1979, 1980, 1982, 1990 by Thomas Nelson, Inc., Nashville, Tennessee.

Published by:

McDougal & Associates
18896 Greenwell Springs Road
Greenwell Springs, Louisiana 70739
www.ThePublishedWord.com

McDougal & Associates is an organization dedicated to the spreading of the Gospel of Jesus Christ to as many people as possible in the shortest time possible.

ISBN 978-1-940461-13-7

Printed on demand in the US, the UK, and Australia
For Worldwide Distribution

DEDICATION

To the many men and women, both living and already gone on before us, who have entrusted their precious manuscripts to me over the years. It has been a privilege serving you, and I hope to serve this new generation for many years to come.

ACKNOWLEDGEMENTS

Writing any book is a big task that requires many hands. Even the content can never be claimed by one single person, as we all learn from each other. This is particularly true of *Publishing and Selling Your Book Made Easy*. This book is the result of many years of working together with others to get the vision of God's people into written form, and many people have blessed me along the way.

I am particularly indebted to Don Nori, Founder of Destiny Image of Shippensburg, Pennsylvania, to Bob Whitaker, Sr., Founder of Whitaker House in New Kensington, Pennsylvania, and to Bishop and Mrs. Dennis Leonard, Founders of Legacy Publishers International of Denver, Colorado. Through these and my own publishing ventures, I have worked on some seven hundred different manuscripts over a period of many years, and you can imagine that I've learned a few things in the process.

Today we can produce quality books and eBooks in record time and at the lowest cost ever. This all benefits God's Kingdom. Our goal is to continue to make the process as painless and economical as possible so that more and more of those who have a story to tell and a message to convey can find their intended audience, and in the process, God can be glorified. My thanks to all who have added their wisdom to these pages.

Other books by Harold McDougal

Principles of Christian Faith
Spanish: *Fundamentos de la fe Cristiana*

The MasterKeys Series:
Speaking in Tongues
Spanish: *Hablando en lenguas desconocidas*
All Things Are Possible
Spanish: *Todo le es posible*
Who We Are in Christ
Spanish: *Quienes somos en Cristo*
Secrets of a Servant
Spanish: *Los secretos de un servidor*

The Rescuing Series:
Rescuing the 21st Century Marriage
Rescuing the 21st Century Teenager

Others:
Laying Biblical Foundations

Out of print books:
I Hugged a Headhunter
Used More Abundantly

More Recent Releases:
I Can Do This
Infallible Proofs
Understanding the Seed [1]*

---

1. With Peter Kange, Jane Lowder and Andy McDougal

CONTENTS

* Are there other areas you would like to see us cover in the future? If so please advise us at publisher@ThePublishedWord.com.

"Harold made the process of transitioning to published Christian writing SO EASY for me. He was helpful at every step. His knowledge of the Scriptures was invaluable. I had no former knowledge of the world of professional publishing, and so everything was new, but Harold made it EASY. He patiently explained each step and the myriad of details. Then he let me respond at my own pace, so that I was not overwhelmed. We have published three books so far with him, and expect another one down the road. I highly recommend McDougal & Associates to anyone who wants to get God's Word out to the world."

Donald C. Mann
Landenberg, Pennsylvania
Author, *Discovering Our Redemption,*
Battle Prayer for Divine Healing
and *OK, God, Now What?*

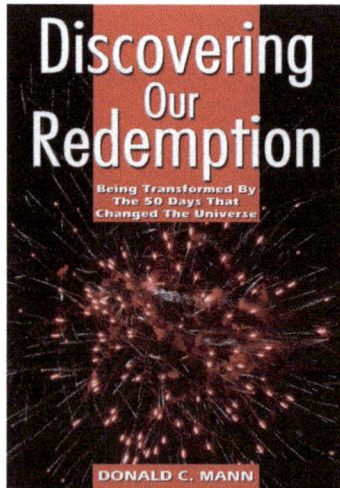

"I would like to express my gratitude for all your hard work, your insight and the professional manner you exhibited in the preparation and publication of my book. You made this journey very EASY for me."

Jody Amato
Pastor, Highway to Heaven
Walker, Louisiana
Author, *Cinderella's Slipper* and *If the Shoe Fits*

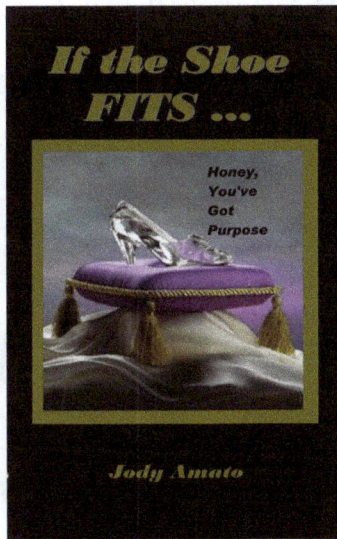

"I have total confidence in you. You're a man of great integrity and efficiency."

John R. Chappell, III
Founder of The Chappell Ministries
Bartow, Florida
Author, *Free from the Past*
and *Living in His Glorious Presence*

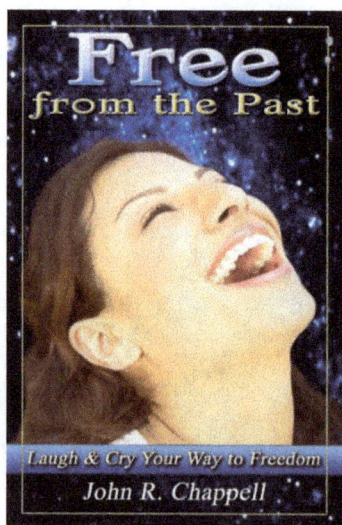

Dear Brother Harold,

*Some people come into our lives and quickly go.
Some people stay awhile and leave footprints on
our hearts, and we are never the same again.
Thank you for stepping into my life.*

Judson Cornwall

Let a man so account of us, as of the ministers of Christ, and stewards of the mysteries of God.

                                           1 Corinthians 4:1, KJV

So look at Apollos and me as mere servants of Christ who have been put in charge of explaining God's mysteries.   *NLT*

So then, let us [apostles] be looked upon as ministering servants of Christ and stewards (trustees) of the mysteries (the secret purposes) of God.   *AMP*

Let a man so consider us, as servants of Christ and stewards of the mysteries of God.   *NKJV*

Introduction

Easy...? Publishing and disseminating a book is no simple matter, for many complex and difficult issues are involved. For the average person, busy with other matters, it is just too much information to digest, and there is no reason that you should have to learn the detail of these issues. That's what we're here for.

However, in our information age, many actually want to understand everything they are doing. So we have prepared the following detailed information for the benefit of those who want to know and understand the many processes.

To make this information as easy as possible to access, we have organized it into frequently asked questions and their answers. Choose an appropriate subject to see a list of all available related materials. When you are finished reading, come back to follow other subjects.

Harold McDougal
Greenwell Springs, Louisiana

"Thank God for the giftings He has invested in His people. I wish to thank Harold McDougal personally for taking this book and making it say what it needed to say. Thanks, Harold, for becoming an extended hand to hear my heart and finish off this work — getting it ready for people out there everywhere."

Andre van Zyl
Good News to the Nations
Dacula, Georgia
Author, *Feed the Camels*
and *Finally, God Makes Sense*

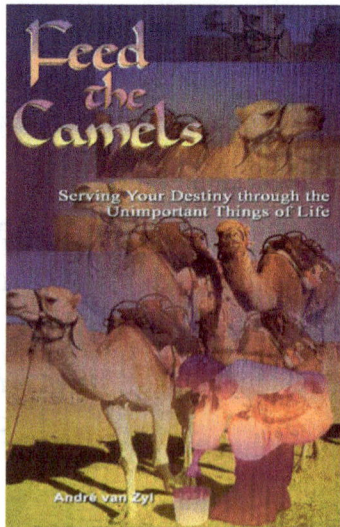

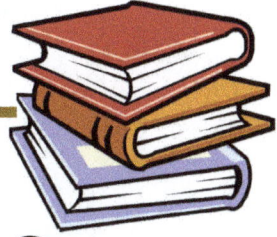

1. The Many Steps in the Publishing Process

There are an amazing number of steps involved in the publishing process. They can be summarized as:

1.1 — The Initial Steps
1.2 — The Creative Steps
1.3 — The Perfecting Steps
1.4 — The Production Steps

How fast a book moves along from concept to actual production depends on the successful coordination of these steps with the author, the publisher, the editor, the typesetter, the cover artist, the proofreader, and the printer. Now that we have Internet communications and can send proof copies by email, what took months or even years in former times can now be accomplished in a matter of a few weeks (or even less). It's a new day!

"His work exceeded my greatest expectations. It was amazing how he was able to capture my heart and express it in the pages of the book, and its message is clear and concise. On a more personal level, Harold is a well-disciplined, industrious man with a pleasant personality."

Lee Edward Gaddie
New Jerusalem Whole Truth Church
Humble, Texas
Author, *The Commander's Anointing*

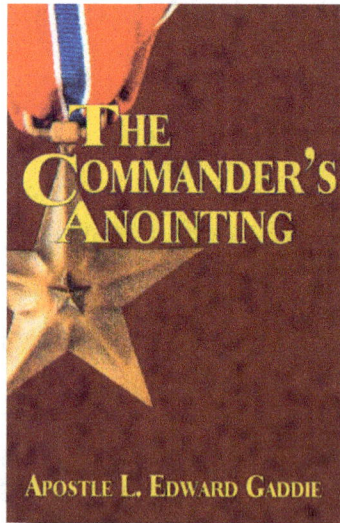

1.1 — THE INITIAL STEPS

The initial steps in the publishing process are technical ones.

- ☐ Contract Submission (author to publisher)

- ☐ Manuscript (or message) Submission (author to publisher)

- ☐ OCR (Optical Character Recognition) if the message is submitted in written form or the Transcribing of Tapes, CDs, or DVDs if the message is submitted in spoken form.

- ☐ File Submission: This previous step can be eliminated when files are submitted digitally, ready for processing. So that is the best way. Submit your files as a Microsoft Word document or a file from one of the other popular word processing programs. Simply attach your file to an email to editor@ThePublishedWord.com.

1.2 — THE CREATIVE STEPS

Some would consider the creative steps the most important. They are:

- ☐ Editing and or Rewriting (this can take the longest of any of the steps, depending on how much editing or rewriting is needed).

- ☐ Typesetting (we now combine these two steps, editing/rewriting and typesetting, into one, working within the editor of the typesetting software to save time and money for the Kingdom). Typesetting includes the preparation of any graphic elements to be included in the book.

- ☐ Cover Design Concept Development

- ☐ Back Cover Text Development

1.3 — THE PERFECTING STEPS

The perfecting steps are important ones. You want your book to be the best it can be, and so do we. In some cases, several rounds of perfecting steps are needed. The perfecting steps are:

- ☐ Cover Design Submission (publisher to author)
- ☐ First Rough Draft Submission (publisher to author)
- ☐ Corrections to the First Rough Draft
- ☐ Changes Needed to the Cover Design
- ☐ Second Text Submission (publisher to author)
- ☐ Second Cover Submission (publisher to author)
- ☐ Proofreading
- ☐ Proofing Changes
- ☐ Submission of the Final Draft
- ☐ Final Text Approval from the Author
- ☐ Submission of the Final Cover Design
- ☐ Final Cover Design Approval from the Author

Within reason, we are willing to do as many rounds of additions and corrections as are needed to prefect the book. However, if these become excessive, some additional charges may be necessary.

1.4 — The Production Steps

When we finally get to the production steps, it is very exciting. A seed was long ago planted in your spiritual womb, and a baby is about to be born. This child has the potential to change the world. The all-important production steps are:

☐ Submission of the Files to the Printer

☐ Printing (Until recent years this was taking 5 weeks or more. Now it can be accomplished in a matter of days for digital processing and ten days to two weeks for offset jobs of 1,500 books or more.

☐ Shipment of the Finished Books

In a former time, an author had to order 3,000 or more books, but now that books are printed digitally and quickly, we advise our authors to order only as many books as they need for the next few months. Then they can order more.

Once you have received your finished books, the real fun begins — distribution of your book to the ends of the earth.

"It seems obvious to me that you are anointed for this type of work. With my many questions, you have taken the time to successfully answer them all. You certainly read my heart as you were editing my manuscript. I am very pleased at how it turned out."

Mary Cummings
Shekinah Ministries
Shreveport, Louisiana
Author *The Restlessness of the Call*
and *People of the Presence*

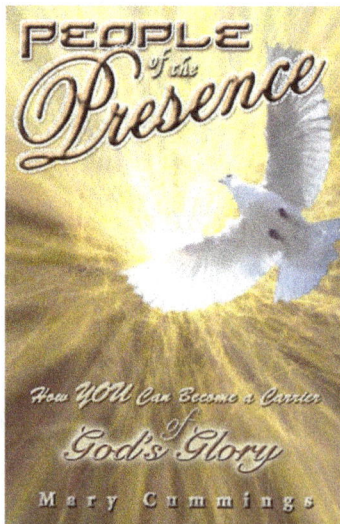

2. QUESTIONS ABOUT THE EDITING PROCESS

Editing is one of the most controversial aspects of Christian publishing. Should an anointed book even be edited? How much or how little editing should be done? And who should do it? etc. Here are the most common questions in this regard:

"With some trembling I approached an author friend for counsel. After all, she had published her first title, which I enjoyed reading, and was working on a sequel. Without hesitation, she recommended Harold McDougal as the man to seek out."

Tommy James
Tree of Life Ministries
Statesville, North Carolina
Author, *Be Reconciled!*

2.1 — Is It Right to Edit Prophetic Material?

This is one of the most common questions I receive from Spirit-filled Christians, and I consider it to be a very important one. First, let's try to define prophetic material. To me, prophetic material is any writing that has a touch of the divine on it. It's anointed. It's life-changing. It came from the very heart of the Father. Usually material such as this is obtained in a public meeting where the anointing is high, and God is doing miracles. If that is true, why, then, would we ever think of editing such materials?

It's a good question, but there's also a good answer. First of all, let me ask if you've ever edited prophetic materials. I believe you have. We all do. Why do I say that? When we have heard from God, we speak forth what He has shown us, and it's powerful. Over time, however, we gain more insight into the matter and realize that we may not have expressed the revelation in the most effective terms. Because there was an aspect of it that we didn't fully understand ourselves, it was not as powerfully presented as it might have been. So, over time, we perfect our revelation, and that is just what editing does.

Editing often has to do with omitting or deleting.

By *omitting*, I mean omitting something controversial that doesn't improve the message or build on it and might even be a distraction for some or for many.

By *deleting* I mean deleting duplicate material or what is known as needless repetition (not to be confused with a style of teaching that uses repetition). I mean taking out the "rabbit trails," the asides that are often added during preaching or teaching. These may have been important for someone who was present when the words were spoken, but they have little or nothing to do with the theme of the book and may well be distracting if left in.

Editing often has to do with rewording.

We reword improper English phrases or words that we all use occasionally (some more than others) but that have no place in a book that we want to reach out to a larger world.

We reword or identify locally used and understood words or phrases that may not be widely understood elsewhere.

We reword or identify slang expressions.

Editing also has to do with adding.

We add transitional words or phrases where they are lacking, causing the flow of the message to be blunted.

We add documentation where it is lacking. This means identifying the source of quoted materials, whether from the Bible itself or from other books. (This can also become a legal issue, meaning that you can be sued for using material without properly recognizing its source. See "What Is Plagiarism, What Is the Penalty for It, and Why Is This So Important for Authors To Understand" under "Questions about Legal Matters," page 97.)

We add biblical notations where appropriate and useful.

We add, in conjunction with the author, any missing element or elements that would leave the book incomplete or ineffective. Usually if it is something short, an editor can add it in the author's style. If it is longer, the author may have to supply it on tape or in a digital file. (For testimonials of our work in this regard, see page 198).

All of these things that we are omitting, rewording, or adding because they are lacking have the effect of weakening a message, so by dealing with them, we are not weakening the message at all. Actually we are strengthening it and making it more understandable and more impactful. That is the most important role of editing.

Editing is for the purpose of improving the flow and impact of the message.

An editor makes sure the message flows from the Introduction through each chapter, climaxing in the final pages and impacting the reader as much as possible. Anything that hinders this flow should be dealt with in the editing process.

There are editors who have no respect for the anointing or for a speaker's or writer's style, and once they have torn the material apart and put it all back together again, it is hardly recognizable as the same message. In this case, the message may, indeed, be weakened. We're not like that. As people who know what it is to have a message from God, we honor every message and only edit one when it will make it even more powerful.

The problem sometimes is that those who spoke the message know how powerful it was when they spoke it, and they wonder, "Why change a message that has been so effective?" The only answer would be: to make it even better, more effective.

2.2 — How Do We Handle the Editing Process?

I approach the editing of the book in three passes:

The First Pass:

During the first pass, I may make some obviously needed changes, but my overall purpose is to acquaint myself with the whole of the material. I make myself some notes as I go along. These concern where various sections seem to fit in the overall picture, what sections seem to be duplication, what sections seem to be anticlimactic, what sections seem to need serious revision or are confusing or seemingly contradictory, what material may be needed to complete the message, etc.

Usually, I also make similar notes to the author during this pass. For instance, I ask questions to clarify some point that has been made in the material. I inquire about the possibility of adding to a point that has not been fully fleshed out. If the material is not well documented, I take this opportunity to inquire about quotations that are used in the book and need documentation, biblical or otherwise. If I can find the biblical quotes (there are so many different translations used these days that this is sometimes a challenge), then I don't have to bother the author with the question of which version they came from. I sometimes send the author a few questions and comments every day when I'm in this pass. That way my inquiries don't become overwhelming for them.

Depending on the size of the book and the quality of the writing, this first pass can take anywhere from a few days to a week or more.

The Second Pass:

In the second pass, I do all the serious editing. I move some things around, delete material that seems to be extraneous, duplication or unhelpful for any other reason. I make any adjustments based on the answers I have received from the author. I sometimes split material into more chapters. I may insert subtitles and select material to be used in pull quotes. At the same time, I also work on things like the best formatting, spacing, graphical usage, etc.

Although I do try to avoid typographical, grammatical and spelling errors, this is not my main focus. During this time (days or weeks) I try to live in the message, feeling the style of the writer and meditating on how best to present it and make it work to his or her advantage.

There is a revelatory element to all of this. During these weeks, I am fully engrossed in the book, talking about it to those around me, dreaming about it at night, always groping in the Spirit for some key that will make the book more powerful, more impactful, something that will leave a lasting memory with those who pick it up. Often this key is hidden somewhere among the "stuff," so to speak. Eventually, at some unexpected point, the secret will be dropped into my spirit. This happens very suddenly and dramatically, and when it does, I sit with tears streaming down my face for a time. I know that, in myself, I did not know the secret for the success of this book, and now I do. I'm very grateful for such a gift.

The Third Pass

The third pass is done over a two- or three-day period. On the first day, I reserve the entire day for this purpose—with no telephones or visitors to distract. I must read through the book (preferably out loud) in one sitting. This can take from 6 to 10 hours or more, depending on the length of the book, the number of times I have to stop to make adjustments, and the severity of those adjustments.

This time is very different. I am sitting down, not in front of my monitor, as I usually am, but in a comfortable chair in some comfortable room and preferably with someone I love and who also loves the message of the Lord and the ministry of books. In this way, we begin to read the hard copy of the book from the title page onward, not skipping anything. We read it as if reading it for the very first time, and we read it as any reader might. We want to see how it will sound to them and what impact it will make on them.

As we read, we move along as quickly as possible, but I pause now and then to make some notation on the page that will allow me to later tweak a sentence, check on a point made or otherwise improve the flow of the message. Whoever is with me will sometimes have a point to make about the message, good or bad. Both are helpful, and I make some notation on the appropriate page to follow up on later.

Invariably we come to pages that don't flow as well as others. I mark these, writing FLOW in big letters on the page. On other pages, I write FOCUS. This part seems to have gotten a little off message and is not focused well enough on the point of the chapter or possibly the theme of the entire book. Later, I can work at making that part more focused.

As I go along, I do check to make sure that the titles of the chapters match the titles as they are written in the table of contents. I also check chapter starting page numbers. But since these technical things will be thoroughly reviewed by a proof-reader before the book goes to press, my concern must always be for the flow of the message and its impact on the reader. Those other things will take care of themselves later. [1]

The reason we need to do this all in one day may not be obvious to everyone. When we get to Chapter 4, the previous three chapters must still be fresh in our minds. This will let us know how the message is flowing or not flowing, what duplication may still exist, which points are working and which are not, etc. By the time we reach the final chapter, we must have in mind all of the previous chapters. That's the only way we can be sure a book is effective.

There are books in which each chapter or section is independent of the others and can stand or fall on its own. These are easier to edit. Each part may or may not need to continue a central theme, and they may or may not build on each other. With most books, however, we must build from the first page to the last, without losing momentum.

When the day is over, we are exhausted but exhilarated. We know that we have made con-siderable improvements to a message that will eventually impact many for the Kingdom of God. It's a good feeling.

---

1. As we have gotten better at avoiding little mistakes, I now sometimes allow an author to have someone they know and trust do the final proofreading of the book if they are concerned about saving money on that part of the project.

To actually sit down before the computer and make the changes we have noted can take the next couple of days. Sometimes I need to consult with the author during this time and sometimes not. Whatever the case, within a couple of days, the first rough draft will go out to the author.

We call it a first rough draft because the author may or may not like it as it stands. Usually that depends on how much they have been involved in its creation. Either way, the ball is now in their court, and they can make any changes they want. The great majority of the people I work with love the first rough draft. They feel that I have captured their spirit, their style, and their message and presented it in the best possible way, and consequently, they have only minor adjustments to make.

Those who make the most changes, ironically, are usually new authors. They don't understand why their original language is not the best way to say things, and they have thought of other things they want to add in the meantime. This can quickly get out of hand. There have been cases where new authors actually doubled the size of the manuscript by adding so much or changing large sections so much that it actually doubled my work. This is not fair to an editor who has agreed to a price to edit a book, and suddenly his workload is doubled, without any additional compensation.

There is another way this review process can be done, and for extremely busy authors, I recommend it. It involves me actually sitting down with the author to do the final polishing procedure. It works like this:

When an author experiences difficulty in finding the necessary time to do a proper final read-through of their manuscript, we can actually arrange a time to sit down together and do it. During the editorial process, we have made slight adjustments, such as adding transitional phrases here and there, rewording some sentences, and focusing the material more around the title or the subject of the book. There are always changes when transferring sermon material into an acceptable book format. When we sit down and read the final draft through together, several things are accomplished:

- ☐ The author hears the book read from a reader's perspective. (This sometimes leads to small changes that can improve the book a lot.)

- ☐ The author is able to see the message in context and to judge it for flow and impact. (This can also lead to positive changes.)

- ☐ Some unnecessary repetition may be noted that weakens the message of the book, and it can be marked to be removed.

☐ As the book is read, the reader can ask for clarification on some minor point, or the author can ask for a little better wording on something that doesn't seem to express exactly the point he or she was trying to make.

☐ When we're done, I always feel so much better because I know that the author is happy with the book as it stands, and I know that it will make the greatest impact possible on the reader. It is then the best book it can be.

Typically, in these sessions, an author will notice sections he's not happy with for one reason or another, and those sections can then be improved. As you can imagine, this all takes time. But it works best when done in the shortest time possible. That way, when we arrive at the final chapter, we still have the context of the first sections in mind.

To do this type of work, we need a quiet place where we will not be disturbed by phone calls or other interruptions, some comfortable chairs so that we can sit for a few hours at a time, and some refreshing drink to keep us hydrated as we work.

If the author wants some other person or persons present in these sessions, to listen and offer suggestions, that's fine, but the author is always the most important person there. It's his (or her) message, and only he (or she) can say what he (or she) meant for sure, so when we are finished, we want him (or her) to be happy with the final product.

The process, again is the following:

I read the book aloud from the beginning to the end, and the author and/or others who are present are able to stop me at any time to ask for a clarification or improvement. From time to time, I may stop and ask for some clarification myself, if I think something could be confusing or if I have any doubt about what the author is saying. English is a complicated language, spoken differently in many places, and we want the book to be understood by the widest possible audience. When we are finished with this process, we have that assurance.

2.3 — What Is the Best Way for the Author to Review a Rough Draft?

Just as I do my work in three passes, the very best way for you, as an author, to review your manuscript on your own is in three passes. In at least one of these stages, you will want to either read it aloud yourself to others or have others read it aloud to you.

Make sure the person who reads it is a good reader. If they stumble over the manuscript, that will not do justice to the message, and it will be hard for you to notice where changes are needed.

The First Read-Through:

In the first round, no serious changes should be made. It's okay to mark sections you want to question later. But the most important point of this first pass is simply to acquaint yourself with the material. If you notice sections that don't flow as well as others, mark them. If you notice sections that seem unnecessarily redundant, mark them, etc.

Try, as much as possible, to do this first pass in one sitting, that is in one day. That way, when you get to the final chapter, the other chapters will still be fresh in your mind.

The Second Read-Through:

Once you have familiarized yourself with the entire book, you can start to make your major changes. This time, you might just want to read problem sections, do some work on them, and then read them again before going on.

For the sake of the editor, make most of your changes on the face of the printout. Use a clearly visible color and texture of ink.

- ☐ **Text to Delete:** Make a mark through something to delete.

- ☐ **Text to Move**: Circle something to move and show with an arrow where it is to be moved.

- ☐ **Text to Add:** Write additions out clearly and show where they are to be added. If an addition is more than a sentence or two, please present it to us typed as a Word file so that we don't have to retype it all again. That's double work for the Kingdom.

2. QUESTIONS ABOUT THE EDITING PROCESS

IMPORTANT: DO NOT RETYPE LARGE SECTIONS OF THE TEXT, including your minor changes. This creates a terrible headache for the editor. When some well-meaning author does this, we must then arduously compare the old text with the new, word by word, to find what has been changed and what is still the same. This is much more than double work. So we must repeat: **PLEASE NO NOT RETYPE LARGE SECTIONS OF YOUR TEXT.** This is one of the most critical mistakes authors can make.

During these read-throughs, although it is not wrong to mark misspelling and grammatical errors for change, this is not your focus. Keep focused on the flow and impact of the message, and don't let anything distract you from it.[2]

The Final Read-Through:

Once you have worked through your major concerns with the book, you're then ready for the final read-through. If at all possible, this read-through should be done aloud, and it should be done in one sitting. To some that would seem impossible, but it's surprising how quickly you can read through a book when you give yourself wholly to it.

2. As noted in an earlier chapter, if an author is concerned about costs and has a friend or close associate he wishes to do the proofing, we sometimes allow it.

If there are things you still question about the manuscript, make some notes with questions for the editor. Together you can work out these final concerns.

2.4 — WHAT ARE YOU LOOKING FOR IN PROOFREADING?

Aside from the usual typographical errors, our proofreaders look for many other things. Here are some of them:

☐ **Title Pages:** On the half-title page and full title page, proofreaders check to make sure the title and subtitle are consistent with each other and with the title and subtitle on the copyright page.

☐ **Copyright Page:** On the copyright page, proofreaders check consistency in the presentation of the copyrights for all the Bible versions used in the book. There are several ways to say it, and sometimes these are copied from other places and get mixed with citations that are worded differently. They also check the ISBN (international standard book number) to make sure it is correct. Once they have read the copyright page through and made sure it is otherwise free of errors, they set it aside to check, as they read through the chapters of the book, that the Bible versions used within the text are documented there. This is an important legal issue.

☐ **Table of Contents:** In the table of contents, proofreaders check the usual spelling and grammar, but they also set this page aside and use it to check that each chapter title agrees with the title as it is written on the content page and that the chapter starting page numbers are correct.

☐ **Consistency:** From the beginning to the end of a particular book, proofreaders check for consistency. In American English, an author can be given a lot of license, but what we must be sure of is that there is consistency throughout each book. For instance, they check for consistency in formatting. If they see anything that doesn't seem consistent, they mark it for change. Vertical spaces missing between Bible verses would be an example of this. Other examples are: some authors use a comma before the final "and" in a series, and some do not. "Fish, meat, and poultry" and "fish, meat and poultry" are both correct, but within a book, we must chose one and stick with it throughout. Using spaces around ellipses and full dashes or not using spaces are both correct. We need consistency in the book. The proofreader makes sure that the first page of every chapter has the same layout and that there is consistency in headers, footers, and page numbers on the other pages. Normally, the left-hand pages (these are even-numbered) should have the book title in italics in the header, and the right-hand pages (these are odd-numbered) should have the chapter title in the header. Footers normally only contain page numbers, but they must be check to see that all pages that should be numbered are numbered and that no blank pages are numbered. Often much of the front matter and/or the back matter is not numbered, but all other pages, except blank pages, should be. If a proofreader sees anything else suspicious in the realm of consistency, they mark it for review or correction.

☐ **Publisher's Irregularities:** Aside from the normal capitalization, we do have some irregularities, as each publisher does. In the secular world, for instance, heaven and hell are never capitalized. We choose to recognize these as real places, just as real as New York, London, and Paris, so we capitalize them always. We also choose to capitalize Word, Scriptures, Book, etc. when they refer to the Bible, God's Word. We capitalize Church when it refers to the universal Body of Christ, and, as you can see, we also capitalize Body when it has the same meaning. Some preachers capitalize everything. To them, the sacredness of the Blood, the Presence of God, the Glory, the Power, God's Hand, etc. are so awesome that they think: how can these not be capitalized? We try to walk a middle line. If not, since our books are about the things of God, nearly every word would have to be capitalized.

☐ **Title and Subtitles:** In all titles and subtitles, proofreaders check to make sure that the rules of capitalization within titles are followed and that there is consistency of format (i.e. font, size, emphasis, etc.) Beyond capitalization and formatting, are there enough subtitles? Too many? Are they well worded? Confusing? Do they capture the thought of the text? Could they be improved? All of this is considered.

☐ **Pull Quotes:** In our books, we sometimes use what are called "pull quotes." Pull quotes are short statements taken from the text of the pages on which they appear. Their purpose is to get and hold the reader's attention (and they work). In odd-numbered chapters, these pull quotes appear on the second page (a left-handed page), then they skip two pages and appear on the next open two pages on the right-hand page. [3] Next, the pull quotes skip two pages and then appear on the left again. In the even-numbered chapters, this reverses. They start first on the right-hand page and switch after skipping two pages. This avoids monotony, and readers seem to like it. Proofreaders must check the pull quotes for positioning (are they on the right page?), for format, and for consistency.

---

3. Both an editor and a proofreader always think of the book as it will open and appear before the eventual reader. The editor works with the two pages visible before him, and the proofreader sometimes lays the pages down on a table before her two pages at a time to get this correct orientation. You can do this too, to get a sense of what your book will look like.

Also, are they meaningful? Will they impact the reader? These are important questions.

- ☐ **Emphasis:** Proofreaders check for too much or improper emphasis. There are many ways to emphasize something that is being expressed in writing: emboldening the font, italicizing it, using all caps, underlining it or a combinations of these. Preachers are great for emphasizing everything, but studies have shown that too much emphasis has a self-defeating effect. The eye is drawn away from the emphasized text, and what registers in the reader's mind as important is the unemphasized text. Quality books, therefore, use NO UNDERLINING at all and very limited italics and bolds. Our policy is as follows: we use as little emphasis as possible, occasionally italicizing words to draw attention to them, never underlining, only very occasionally using bolds. We feel that an occasional use of italics and all caps is sufficient emphasis. Since our scripture verses are italicized (and, in some cases, also emboldened), we usually use only all caps for emphasis within

a quoted verse, and then we insert
the notation "Emphasis Added," or
"Emphasis Mine." Italics especially have
some important legitimate uses within
a book. For instance, book titles, movie
titles, and magazine names are italicized.
Foreign words are italicized. When
referring to a particular English word,
that word is italicized. For example:
"This word *fight,* according to *Strong's,*
has the meaning of ... . " Aside from
checking to be sure that all legitimate
uses of emphasis are met, proofreaders
are free to voice an opinion about too
much or too little emphasis.

☐ **Scripture Quotations:** In all scripture
quotations, proofreaders check to see
that the passage is from the correct
version. If it doesn't have a version
notation—KJV, NAS, NIV, etc.—then
it must be from the version specified
on the copyright page as the principle
version for the book. If a version other
than the principle version noted on the
copyright page is used, the proofreader
must go back and check to see that the
version quoted is properly documented
on the copyright page. If not, she makes

a notation there to add it. This is an
important legal matter, and we want
to avoid lawsuits. There are so many
versions available now that it would be
difficult for every proofreader to keep a
copy of each one on hand. Fortunately,
many versions are now available
online. Proofreaders also check all Bible
quotations for correctness. When I place
a verse these days, I generate it from
the Internet (as long as I can find the
version being quoted), so there are no
mistakes in it, but if the author generated
the verses by hand or spoke them from
memory, then there is room for error.
Beyond these obvious things, is a verse
relevant within the context? Does it add
to the message? Could it, perhaps, be
shortened or eliminated without losing
anything from the message? Some
authors like to add comments within the
biblical text. Since most Bible translations
don't use square brackets [ ], we usually
use them to show editorial content
within quotes. The problem comes when
an author uses the Amplified version,
which does use square brackets. In that

case, we change to curly brackets { } for editorial comment within the quote.

- ☐ **Punctuation, Grammar, and Spelling**: Punctuation, grammar and spelling errors do occur. Like everyone else, we make mistakes, and it is not uncommon for a proofreader to find four or more mistakes per page. Some pages may have none, and other pages may have quite a few. A gifted proofreader will spot them, when neither we nor the author have.

- ☐ **The Broader View:** Beyond the normal search for grammatical and punctuation errors, we need a proofreader to take on the role of looking at the material from the aspect of a potential reader. We never mind it when a proofreader makes a notation such as: "this is confusing," "this could be misunderstood," or "this seems contradictory." Normally, such a decision would be considered an editorial one, but we find this extremely helpful, so we welcome it. The author is too close to the writing, and we editors sometimes have the same problem. Proofreaders sometimes find things obviously wrong with a manuscript when neither of us noticed. It never hurts for them to make a suggestion. As the editor and publisher, I have the final word, so, on the final copy, I only make the changes I agree with. If a proofreader feels very strongly about something, I tell them to note is as a statement. If they're not sure, but think something might improve the writing or its impact on the reader, I tell them to make their notation into a question. "Would it be better ...?"

☐ **Style:** Proofreaders check for consistency in style. In our books, we use the novel (or conversational style) of writing. This does a couple of important things: (1) It makes our books very easy to read, and (2) It gives our authors the liberty they need to express themselves. However, there are two things we have to guard against: (1) Preachers have the tendency to put words on paper the same way they would say them to an audience, and that doesn't always work in a book. This is the largest area of criticism of tape-to-book projects, and we have no reason to give the critics of the things of the Spirit any ammunition to use against us. If it sounds like a sermon, it needs rewording. When someone is preaching, they rely not only on words, but on hand and facial gestures. They may point to something or hold up something in the sight of the audience. They can use pauses. They can raise their voice or lower it. They can jump, run, or move in some other way. In a book, we have none of these helps. Every word must stand on its own. We cannot insert "grin" as many do in emails these days. (2) When several people work on a book, there is the danger of having several different styles mixed. I try to change as little as possible so that we can preserve the author's style. If something seems out of character, I ask proofreaders to note it, and then I deal with it.

☐ **Stilted, Formal, and Complicated Language:** Proofreaders look for stilted, formal or complicated language. College-level writing restraints have a purpose, and that is to get a student to express him- or herself in the most precise and correct way, but what they write isn't always very interesting to read. Many college graduates are very proud of their dissertation, but few dissertations find their way into book form. They're too boring. If a book sounds too scholarly, it turns people off. Textbook-type books don't sell well in the Christian arena. There's another reason to keep a book simple. Studies show that the average American still reads at the sixth- to tenth-grade level. Because of this, I insist on simple sentences, simple paragraphs and down-to-earth wording. Another good reason to keep our books simple and to the point is that they go all over the world, and a great percentage of the people who read them in other countries have English as a second (or even third) language. For their sake, we simply must keep the message simple and easy to understand. At college level, a sentence never begins with "and" or "but." BUT, in the real world, that's the way we talk. Reading popular novels can help a writer get the idea of more informal language. At the college level, many words that we commonly use are considered archaic. In fact, college-level grammar-checking programs find most of the Bible to be archaic and wordy. In expressing the Gospel, we use what the world considers to be archaic and wordy language. It is, however, the language of the heart. When a man wants to tell his fiancé that he loves her, all thought of college-level English grammar and punctuation rules go out the window, and he speaks from his heart. That's how we want our books to read. At the college level, you never end a sentence with a preposition. In the real world, it's done all the time. Not doing it leaves you with a "stilted" phraseology that most people don't enjoy reading.

☐ **Unique Considerations:** Proofreaders look for things unique to book writing. In most kinds of writing, the ending quotation marks can sometimes appear inside the final period of the sentence, but this is never done in books. The ending quotation marks always appear outside.

☐ **Number Formatting:** Numbers also are handled differently in magazines and books. We write numbers out when possible. There are some complicated rules for formatting money and numbers within quoted material. Proofreaders check them all.

Proofreaders consult a style manual when necessary, and that is often because there are so many thousands of decisions to be made in regard to how to present certain text. For the most part, we use the classic *Chicago Manual of Style, 15th Edition.* All of this is designed to present the Word of our Lord given through you in the best possible light. He deserves that, and so do you, as His spokesperson.

3. QUESTIONS ABOUT THE COVER-DESIGNING PROCESS

"I wholeheartedly thank McDougal & Associates for the guidance and expertise that was provided with publishing my book. Brother McDougal was able to transform vision and inspired writing into a devotional-style workbook guaranteed to equip Christians to reach out to the world around them."

Susan Skelley
Daytona Shores Beach, Florida
Author, *Awakening to the Heartbeat of God*

3.1 — WHAT DO WE LOOK FOR IN A GOOD BOOK COVER?

Designing a successful cover for a book requires combining artistic skill with spiritual insight. We, therefore, don't use secular designers at all. Our designers pray about the message and sometimes read the Introduction and table of contents (or even more of the material) before the book is fully finished, to try to capture the essence of the message in the cover design. That design must be attractive enough to draw potential readers, and it must speak to the subject of the book.

A cover is everything. Should you judge as book by its cover? Absolutely! Everyone does.

3.2 — WHAT TYPE OF ARTISTS DO WE WORK WITH?

The cover artists we work with are also in ministry. They pray about the theme of the book and come up with some cover concepts they feel will be suitable (usually no more than two or three).

We look at those concepts and also send them to the author (these days as PDF files or JPEGs) to be viewed and commented on. Then we tell the artist what we like and don't like about her original ideas, and she makes the necessary adjustments to come up with a design suitable to all.

Since we pay our artists so little (they, like us, are doing their work as a ministry), we always hope that we can agree on a cover design as painlessly as possible. Two or three rounds of adjustments should be the limit. Over that, and we're imposing on her good graces.

3.3 — What Is the Cover-Designing Process?

We supply the artist with some information on the book. She prays about it and comes up with several (usually no more than 2 or 3) front cover concepts. We send these to the author, and we look them over ourselves. Between us, we give her enough feedback to help her perfect the design we feel comes closest to meeting our mutual needs.

When we are getting close to a final front cover design, we ask the author for bio information and a photo suitable for the back cover. With that in hand, we write a proposed back cover text and submit it to the author. Through author feedback, we are able to polish the back cover text.

When the back cover text has been agreed upon, we forward it to the artist so that she can then supply us with a full cover design. This will include front, back, and spine (with corresponding title, author's name and logo). Once the full cover has been approved, we are ready to process and upload the needed files to the printer.

3.4 — WHAT IMPORTANCE DOES THE BACK COVER HAVE?

The back cover of a book may not seem all that important, but it can actually make or break the book. Exhaustive studies have been done about what a prospective reader looks at. First, it's the front cover. If that appeals to her, she then turns the book over and reads what's on the back. If that gets her attention, she'll look at the table of contents and Introduction, but if not, she'll put the book down and move on. Therefore:

- □ The back cover text must be short, to the point and targeted.

- □ The author's photo must be of good quality.

- □ The author's bio cannot be wordy or boring.

- □ The design of the back cover, although much less important, should pleasantly combine with the front cover. Fonts should be easy to read and not too many different ones should be used.

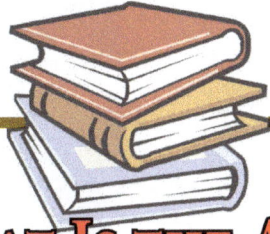

3.5 — WHAT IS THE AUTHOR'S PART IN ALL OF THIS?

Many authors have a definite idea about what they want to portray on the front cover. This may be good, but more often it can be a serious hindrance. Authors are not necessarily artistic, and although they might know when something looks good or not, they can't always tell someone what to do to make it look exactly as they would like it. In these cases, authors should trust the artist's tastes. If an endless round of changes is ordered up to the cover, this becomes burdensome for everyone, pushes the project far beyond its original budget, and can easily delay the release of the book.

The author's part, therefore, is to quickly turn around the cover proofs, making any suggestions in a clear and understandable way. "I just don't like it," is not a very helpful critique. Help the artist to know what to do to make it acceptable. More than just your own tastes are in play. Let a few potential readers look at it and get their opinions. It is, after all, readers who will be buying the book.

"When the Lord commissioned me to write a book, I was willing to step out in faith and obey, but I didn't know where to begin. The Lord, however, is faithful, and He directed my footsteps in this walk of faith, introducing me to this mighty man who became my publisher."

David Jones
Little David Ministries
Charlotte, North Carolina
Author, *Humble Is the Way*

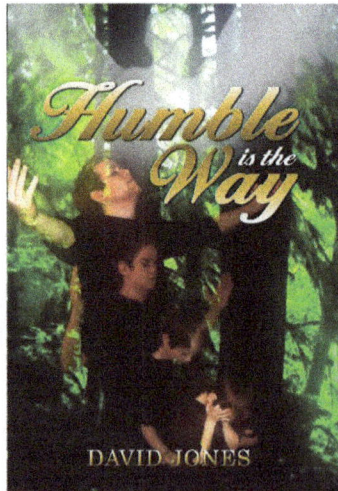

4. Questions About the Printing Process

"I now know why ... seeking Harold to do my publishing was so important. I was not disappointed with my books, my relationship with McDougal & Associates or the professional and affordable manner in which the books were produced. If you choose McDougal & Associates, when your book publishing experience is over, you'll have more than a superb, top quality printing; you'll have a friend for life!"

Eddie T. Rogers,
Revival In Power,
LaGrange, Georgia
Author, *The Power of Impartation*
and *Supernatural*

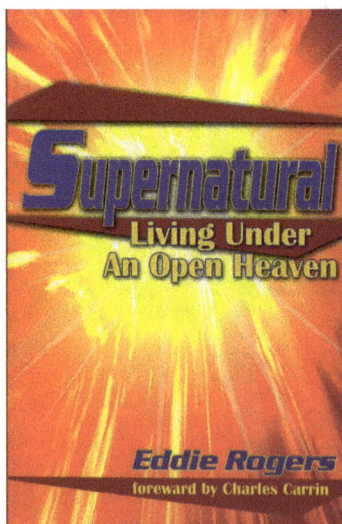

4.1 — WHAT'S NEW IN THE BOOK PRINTING PROCESS?

The printing process has changed dramatically in recent years. We are now using a state-of-the-art process that produces and ships a high-quality book within 48 hours of receiving the order. In this process, there is no plate and no negatives. It's all digital. This means cheaper printing, faster printing, and the ability to make changes needed in a book at any point in time.

It also means being able to order smaller quantities at one time and to reorder as many times as necessary. We call this process POD or Print-on-Demand.

4.2 — What Is POD, or Print-on-Demand?

What do we mean by on-demand printing? It's simple. Today's technology allows us to order any number of your books at one time — even a single book, if that's all you need at the moment. The amazing thing about all of this is:

- ☐ The cost is not prohibitive, as it was before.
- ☐ The quality is excellent, rivaling books done on any printing system.

This is why we call this new technology revolutionary! It's one of the true marvels of the twenty-first century, and now we can use it for the Gospel and for getting YOUR message out.

4.3 — What Are the Costs Involved in Doing On-Demand Publishing?

The costs of doing a book POD are surprisingly small:

☐ **Printer's Setup Fee:** There is a one-time printer setup fee of $100.00, and an annual LSI Marketing Access Fee of $12. This fee is to maintain your title in the LSI system and make it available to wholesalers and retailers. [4]

☐ **Proof Fee:** If you require a physical proof, there is a fee of $30 (this includes overnight shipping). For hardback books, the physical proof cost is $35. If no physical copy is required, we review an online proof and the approve the title for production.

---

4. As of January 1, 2015, there will be a $3 Publisher's Surcharge attached to this fee to help us maintain the title on our own site.

☐ **Cost Per Copy:** After the initial setup, your charges will be per copy for the number of books you order (plus a 10% Publisher's Surcharge). The printing cost of each book can vary from $1.54 and up, depending on the size and type, plus actual shipping costs and any related state and county taxes. Email us for specific quotes.

If you can use 1,500 or more copies of your book, we can get excellent offset press quotes with much better prices, and for quantities of 2,500 and more the digital prices are better than the offset prices and shipping costs improve, as well. Let us give you a quote today. As noted, our POD partner is Lighting Source International (LSI), with printing facilities in the U.S., the U.K., and Australia.

4.4 — WHAT IS LIGHTNING SOURCE?

Our printing partner is LSI, Lightning Source International. Some years ago now, the very large company known as Ingram Books bought out Spring Arbor, the largest Christian book distribution in the world at the time, making Ingram the largest. It was Ingram that began this new service called Lightning Source International, or LSI for short. LSI uses a new type of digital press (operating in the US [near Nashville, in eastern Pennsylvania, and in Bakersfield, California], in the UK [near London] and in Australia) to print, bind, and ship a book within 48 hours of it being ordered. In this way, these books can be shipped out to anywhere in the world.

At first, this service was utilized for out-of-print titles, making them available again to the general public. Then some publishers began using LSI's digital short-run services for trial runs or test marketing of their new books. This proved to be very successful. Eventually small publishers like us discovered LSI. Now use of this phenomenal service has literally gone through the roof in recent years. And with reason. The quality of LSI books is absolutely wonderful, unlike early digitally printed editions. Since LSI also has digital presses in the UK and Australia, books can be quickly printed and shipped to customers anywhere in the world. To our way of thinking, Lightning Source is God's gift to the ministry.

4.5 — What Is the LSI Setup Process?

Before LSI can print our books or make them available to bookstores, distributors or online retailers, we first have to set up each title in their system. This involves identifying the title and/or subtitle, author, ISBN, major themes, the retail price (in dollars for the U.S., in British Pounds for the U.K., in Euros for the rest of Europe, and in Australian dollars for Australia), the allowable discounts (we usually go with 40% as most bookstores the world over need that much to exist) and the return policy. We accept no returns because 1.) We don't have the staff to handle them, and 2.) It becomes very expensive.

Once the book is set up in the LSI system, we then upload the corresponding text and cover files in their respective formats. If required, we can have them send us an actual printed copy of the book as a proof. (The additional cost is $30 including overnight shipping, $35 for hardback versions.) But we can also now view our proofs online. In either case, once the proof has been approved, the book is ready to release to the author, and also resellers, both wholesale and retail.

4.6 — How Does the POD System Work?

Once the setup process is finished, your book files reside in the LSI system and the book can be ordered through any number of online retailers. When a book is sold, a report of that sale comes to us at the end of the month, and the payment for it comes in 90 days. We report sales and disburse monies to our authors quarterly.

An order of books for yourself must be submitted to us through email (or phone call), and then we submit it to LSI online, paying in advance. We, therefore, need your payment in advance. You can order any number of books, and they will be printed, bound, and shipped anywhere in the world, usually within 48 hours.

Please take note: To cover themselves, LSI advises us to allow 10 days for an order of books (5 days for printing and 5 days for UPS shipping). Our experience is that most orders take much less time. Occasionally LSI gets overly busy and takes the full ten days.

The cost of each book is from $1.54 up, depending on the size of the book and the number of pages. We pay LSI, and then we bill you the exact amount of their charges, plus a surcharge of 10% to cover our expenses. There is also a $15 order fee. For those who need books more quickly, LSI offers an express service. It costs 10% more. There are faster shipping options, but since books are heavy, this gets very expensive.

For most orders, we recommend UPS Ground. USPS service is available for quantities of 25 or less. [5]

---

5. Shipping options vary with printing location.

4.7 — WHAT ARE THE ADVANTAGES OF THE POD SYSTEM?

There are many advantages with the Print-On-Demand system:

□ **IT'S QUICK:** Your books can ship within 48 hours of us placing the order.

□ **THERE'S NO INVENTORY TO STORE:** Now you order only what you need for the immediate future because you can order more at any time, and there's therefore no need to keep more on hand than you can actually use.

□ **IT'S LESS EXPENSIVE:** Although on-demand copies of a book in small quantities typically cost about twice what you would pay if you were printing thousands of copies at one time, if you can't use thousands of copies, then ordering more is just wasteful. In the end, therefore, this system comes out costing you less.

☐ **YOUR EXPENSES ARE SPACED OUT MORE:** Because you order only what you can use in the immediate future and then order more when you need them, your total expenses are spread out over a much longer period of time.

☐ **YOU CAN AVOID PACKING AND SHIPPING:** Instead of packing and shipping your books to a given location for some special event, let us order them directly from the printer and have them shipped to the location where they will be needed.

☐ **YOU GET DISTRIBUTION:** Once your book is in the POD system, it automatically becomes available on Amazon.com, BN.com, and many other web sites for online ordering. It also becomes available to brick and mortar bookstores everywhere through Ingram Wholesale and Baker & Taylor. When anyone orders a book, it is billed, produced and shipped to them (without you doing anything at all). At the end of each month, all sales are reported to us, and at the end of 90 days, payment is received. We report sales and disperse earnings to our authors quarterly. [6] The amount each author receives is the difference between the wholesale price of the book and the production cost for that particular copy, minus 10% Publisher's Discount. Having your book in the POD system cannot guarantee that it will sell, but at the very least this gets it out there to the general public. [7]

☐ **YOUR BOOK CAN BE EASILY REVISED AND UPDATED:** Because the process is all digital and there are no expensive negatives and printing plates involved, the files that are used to produce your book can be revised and/ or updated at any time and as often as you would like. This is very important to some authors. [8]

6. Since LSI pays us 90 days after sales are reported, our payments to authors are one quarter behind sales reports. In other words, the sales reports go out at the end of one quarter, and the corresponding payments go out the end of the next quarter.
7. There is a $15 per year marketing access fee that makes this all possible, $12 charged by LSI and $# by McDougal & Associates.
8. LSI charges a $40 fee for the placement of each revised file, and $35 hourly rates may apply to text and cover changes and the reprocessing and uploading of the new files.

To summarize:

- ☐ **Amazingly Quick Service:** Books can be printed and shipped in as little as 48 hours.

- ☐ **Only What Is Needed:** We no long have to print thousands of books at a time. We can order 10 if that's all that are needed right now.

- ☐ **No More Costly Warehousing of Books:** LSI will print and ship books anywhere for us.

- ☐ **Books Shipped to Any Location:** We can order and have books shipped to any location where special meetings will be held. [9]

- ☐ **Excellent Quality**

- ☐ **Very Decent Prices**

- ☐ **Distribution:** This is achieved through the largest booksellers in the world and to bookstores everywhere through the major distributors.

---

9. LSI advises us to allow 10 days, 5 days for printing and 5 days for UPS ground shipping. Also, if you send a check, we need a day for it to clear. If you pay by credit card, that can take 4 to 5 business days to be credited to our account

Here's how LSI says it on their web site:

- ☐ Quality Book Manufacturing
- ☐ Multiple Order and Delivery Options
- ☐ Access to the Largest Bookselling Channel in the Industry
- ☐ Efficient Inventory Management
- ☐ Lightning Print to Order
- ☐ Wholesale Distribution
- ☐ eBooks Delivered in the Most Popular Formats
- ☐ Service in the US, the UK and Australia

And all of this is now at your service, to enable your message to reach more markets. What could be more wonderful!

4.8 — How Can LSI Help with Distribution?

The production part of the LSI POD service is wonderful, but the distribution part is just as wonderful. Far too many authors have produced books, thousands of them, and then not been able to sell them, and those unsold books are still sitting in some closet or basement or have been stuffed under some bed. Distribution is a hard job, with many important facets. We need access to the online booksellers, and we need access to Christian bookstores. LSI gives us both of these, and they take care of the details.

When a book goes on sale at LSI, it is automatically picked up by the online retailers and automatically becomes available to any brick and mortar bookstore through book distributors. When our authors Google their title, they are amazed at how many resellers list their book. Many of them pick up their feed from Amazon.

This, of course, does not guarantee that anyone will ask for your book either in a bookstore or online. That will require some promotion on your part. Those authors who get involved in promoting their own book or books do well with sales. Those who don't can't expect to sell books, for no one even knows their book exists. That said, getting your title out into the public eye is worth the small cost involved. [10]

When anyone orders a book through a reseller, that reseller takes care of billing and collecting the payment. They pass the order to LSI, and the book is printed, bound, and shipped. At the end of each month, we receive a report of how many books have sold (though not *who* has sold them), and the payment is received in 90 days.

What LSI pays is the difference between the wholesale price of the book and the cost of producing it. The wholesale is typically 60% of retail. For example, if you had a $20 book and the cost of printing it was $3.50 per copy, LSI would pay $12 - $3.50 or $8.50 for each book sold. To my way of thinking, this is a GREAT deal. [11]

According to the latest LSI data, the following are their distribution partners:

IN THE UNITED STATES

Ingram Distributors, Amazon.com, Baker & Taylor, Barnes & Noble, NACSCORP and Expresso Book Machine.

---

10. LSI charges $12 a year to maintain this distribution service for each title and, as of January 1, 2015, McDougal & Associates will add to that a $3 annual fee to help defray our own web costs.

11. As of January 1, 2015, McDougal & Associates will deduct 10% before passing it along to the authors.

IN EUROPE

Adlibris, Agapea, Amazon.com, Aphrohead, Bertrams, Blackwell, Book Depository Ltd., Books Express, Coutts Information Services Ltd., Design-arta Books, Eden Interactive Ltd., Gardners, Trust Media Distribution (formerly STL), Mallory International, Paperback Shop Ltd., Superbookdeals, The Book Community Ltd., W&G Foyle Ltd., and Wrap Distribution.

IN AUSTRALIA AND NEW ZEALAND

Rainbow Book Agencies, The Nile, ALS, Biblioquest, Booktopia, DA Information Services, Dennis Jones & Associates, Footprint Books, Garrat Publishing, Holistic Page, James Bennett, Koorong, Peter Pal, University Co-operative Bookshop, Westbooks and Wheelers NZ.

4.9 — How Much Does McDougal & Associates Earn on Each Book?

For the first ten years of our existence in this POD system, unlike other publishers, we did not place any markup on printing costs. What LSI charged is what our authors paid, not a penny more. As of January 1, 2015, because of the increased work involved in managing so many titles, we began placing a surcharge of just 10% over printer costs to help us defray the expenses involved.

4.10 — CAN LSI HELP WITH eBOOKS?

LSI helps us with two types of eBooks. They are authorized aggregators for Apple iBooks, so we upload our iBook versions to them and they report sales to us monthly.

LSI is also a distributor of eBooks in the formerly most popular Adobe Reader (or Adobe Digital Editions) version. We register these titles with them, upload the Adobe version to their site (where they are released to a large number of online retailers of eBooks, and they report sales to us monthly. In another section, I have a list of resellers currently served by LSI (see pages 170-172).

Since eBooks is now a subject unto itself, please see my notes elsewhere on digital editions (pages 161-182).

4.11 — Does LSI Do Offset Printing?

For orders of 1,500 or more books, LSI partners with offset printers to provide us better pricing. Even using offset, there are advantages for going with LSI:

- **Quick Service:** You must get in line a least a month in advance with a typical offset printer, but an LSI offset order takes only ten days to two weeks to ship (usually less).

- **Distribution:** A typical offset printer can produce your books, but they cannot provide you with distribution. With LSI, you're in the distribution system.

- **Digital Options:** If the LSI digital presses are not busy, sometimes they opt to print our large orders digitally (and that means even faster service). On orders of 2,500 ore more copies, digital presses are now competitive with traditional offset.

4.12 — Does LSI Offer Any Volume Discounts?

Years ago, LSI effectively lowered their prices by instituting the following volume discounts, that still stand today:

Units Ordered	Volume Discount
100-249	10%
250-499	20%
500+	25%

12

If you don't need more books and don't have extra cash lying around, we recommend that you order only as many books as you can use in the next few months. That's the beauty of this system.

If you need more books, not only do larger orders merit larger discounts; the shipping is also cheaper. It costs about as much to ship 500 books as it does to ship 1,000.

---

12. These discounts apply to a single order shipped to a single address, not to split orders.

4.13 — How Quickly Can You Get Your Books

This is the all-important question every author asks, and the answer is this:

Once you approve your final text and cover, the corresponding files will then be uploaded to LSI. If a proof copy is required, it typically arrives in about 5 days. In the past, we always had a proof copy shipped to us so that we could examine it carefully and make sure everything was as it should be. Now, however, we can view the proof online. Once that title is marked as approved on the LSI site, it is ready for production. If you have already placed an order, it will be processed immediately. If not, you should decide and advise us how many copies you want in the first printing and where to ship them.

When an order is placed, LSI suggests that you allow 10 working days to receive your books (5 days for printing and 5 days for UPS Ground shipping). We've found that it usually takes less. To be on the safe side, order your books at least 2 weeks before you will need them.

4.14 — How Do You Order and Pay for More Books?

Your Order/s

Unfortunately LSI only deals with publishers, so you need to send your order to us (if possible at least two weeks before you actually need the books). You can do this by email (orders@The-PublishedWord.com) or by phone (225-262-1937). Emailing your order is the most convenient method for us. In your communication, let us know the following:

1. How many books to order
2. Where and how the books are to be shipped [13]
3. How you would like to pay

The reason it is important to give us the shipping address is that the LSI online order form requires the method of shipping before they will quote a price.

---

13. Shipping is more economical if you order by case lots. Once your title has been registered with LSI, we can supply you with case lot figures.

The shipping alternatives for books from LSI are USPS (for small orders of books, 25 or less), UPS Ground (for most orders) and commercial truck for larger orders. Second Day Air and Overnight are available, but books are so heavy that shipping them this way becomes unreasonably expensive. We are always happy to give you quotes on varying amounts of books, so that you can decide how many you need to order.

Your Payment/s

When we began in 2004, we had so few authors that we could order the books, pay in advance, and then bill the author as a 30-day business account. This is no longer possible. We have so many orders now that we need your payment in advance.

Your payment options are:

☐ Send Us a Check [14]

☐ Pay by Credit Card [15]

Notifications

14. Make your check payable to McDougal & Associates, 18896 Greenwell Springs Road, Greenwell Springs, LA 70739. We will deposit your check and place the order the next day.

15. If you pay by credit card, we must pass along to you the 2.5 % processing fee, and we strongly urge that you give us information from one credit card to keep on file so that you do not need to send sensitive information in an email. With credit card transactions, it takes 4 to 5 business days for the funds to be deposited in our account.

4. QUESTIONS ABOUT THE PRINTING PROCESS

We will notify you by email: (1) When your order has been placed and (2) When we receive the ship notification from LSI and will include the corresponding tracking numbers. [16]

---

16. Orders shipped by USPS are not trackable.

"I deeply appreciate the outstanding service you provided. You made it so easy and a lot less stressful than I imagined. You interacted with me throughout the process, and that was very encouraging. You are very knowledgeable and professional and seemed genuinely interested in helping me accomplish this kingdom assignment. Because of your efforts, I am able to get my message out to the world, and I am very satisfied with choosing you as my publisher. I will continue to use your services in the future, as well as recommend you to others."

Pastor Robert Kendrick
Baton Rouge, Louisiana
Author, *Lord, Help Me! I'm "Failing" in Love!*

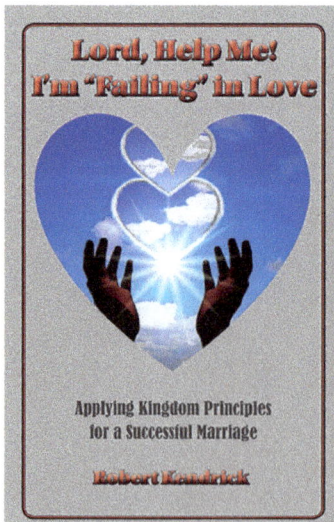

5. QUESTIONS ABOUT LEGAL MATTERS

5.1 — What Is an ISBN?

5.2 — What Is an EAN Barcode?

5.3 — Who Holds the Copyright to Your Book?

5.4 — Who Owns the Exclusive Rights to Your Book?

5.5 — What Is Plagiarism, What Is the Penalty for It, and Why Is this So Important for Authors to Understand?

5.6 — What Is Documentation in a Book?

5.7 — What Is the Purpose of a Copyright Page?

5.8 — What Are Royalties and Will You Receive Them?

5.9 — What Does a McDougal & Associates Publishing Contract Look Like?

"As a first-time writer I was incredibly nervous about finding a publisher and I cried out to God that He would lead me to someone whom I could trust and feel safe with. He answered my prayers by leading me to Harold McDougal. From the start Harold treated me with respect and kindness, despite my being so new in the whole writing process. I was thoroughly blessed by his wonderful combination of profession-alism, integrity and sensitivity to the Holy Spirit. I would warmly recommend him as a seasoned and gifted publisher and see it is an as honor that I was able to work together with him on my book."

Amanda Goransson, Gothenburg, Sweden
Author: *Warrior Women, Arise*

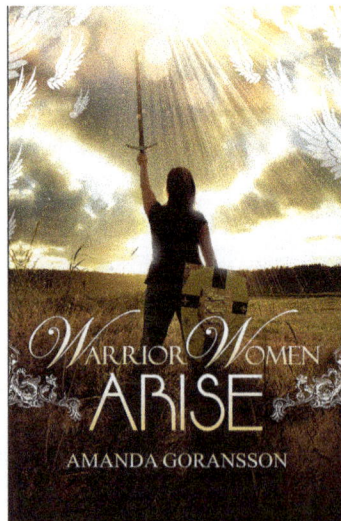

5.1 — WHAT IS AN ISBN?

An ISBN is an International Standard Book Number. This is a system set up to identify books worldwide. All books handled by bookstores must have a unique ISBN. Each edition of a book — a hardback edition, an e-Book edition, an audio edition, etc. — must have a unique ISBN.

McDougal & Associates has been assigned a block of ISBNs by the agency controlling their issue and we assign one of our numbers to each book during the production process. Once a book is published, the details for that title are provided to the agency so that they are then known everywhere.

5.2 — WHAT IS AN EAN BARCODE?

An EAN barcode is a machine-readable code used to process books in bookstores worldwide. Distributors will no longer handle a book that does not bear an EAN barcode on its back cover. If they have to place a sticker on the book with the corresponding barcode on it, they charge extra for that service.

Secular books, sold in supermarkets and drug stores, bear a different barcode. Sometimes a second barcode is printed inside the front cover. Since the EAN barcode is the most widely used barcode in the book industry, we use it exclusively.

Although we have the ability to produce our own barcodes, Lightning Source does it for us, as part of their cover template service, and this assures accuracy. Some barcodes, if not properly designed and printed, will not work.

Barcodes not only identify the ISBN of the book. They also identify the country that particular book is authorized for and the retail price. Since our books sell in many countries, we use the code which indicates that they are for sale anywhere, and we also do not place any retail price on them because:

☐   It allows retailers to set their own price.

☐   It allows for a later price rise without the redesign of the cover.

☐   It allows the author to charge more in ministry situations.

5.3 — WHO HOLDS THE COPYRIGHT TO YOUR BOOK?

Unless otherwise indicated in your contract, you hold the copyright to your book. When the book is published, it bears the copyright symbol on the copyright page, and that protects you. For additional protection, we file a copyright application in your name, presenting two copies of your already-printed book to the U.S. Registrar of Copyrights. Within a couple of months after publication, a certificate of copyright is returned to us and will then be mailed to you for your files.

5.4 — WHO OWNS THE EXCLUSIVE RIGHTS TO YOUR BOOK?

Unless otherwise specified in your contract, you hold exclusive rights to your book, meaning that you can, at any time, withdraw it from circulation, make a contract with another publisher, decide to do some other edition of it, revise and reprint it, etc.

5.5 — WHAT IS PLAGIARISM, WHAT IS THE PENALTY FOR IT, AND WHY IS THIS SO IMPORTANT FOR AUTHORS TO UNDERSTAND?

According to Wikipedia, the online dictionary, plagiarism is "the practice of claiming or implying original authorship of (or incorporating material from) someone else's written or creative work, in whole or in part, into one's own without adequate acknowledgement." [17] In more simple terms, plagiarism is copying someone else's material without acknowledging them as the source. This is a serious criminal offense with serious financial and criminal consequences ($100,000 fine for the first occurrence and fines for every copy of your book that contains plagiarized material), and therefore each author needs to know what is involved and how to avoid it.

What does this mean in practical terms for your book? It means that when you quote from someone else's material found in books, magazines or

17. http://en.wikipedia.org/wiki/Plagiarism

online sources, you must enclose the material in quotation marks and then document it. Because so much material is now available for study on the Internet, many well-meaning people incorporate parts of someone else's writing into their own, without documenting where they got it. This is VERY DANGEROUS and puts you at potential legal risk. [18]

---

18. For information on how to properly document quoted material, see the next section.

5.6 — What Is Documentation in a Book?

When you quote someone, you must document that quote. That documentation gives the person who said it credit for the quote, and this protects you from lawsuits.

For a quote from a book, for instance, you must give the author's name, the title of the book, the publisher, and the year and place of publication. For a magazine, you must give the author, title, number of the issue, etc. For online material, you must give the website address, with all of its extensions.

Even Bible verses must be documented. If you use the New King James Version of the Bible, for example, and your principle version for the book is some other version (the principle version is the one you use more than any others), then on the page where the New King James quote appears, you must identify it as being NKJV, and on the copyright page, you must include the copyright information for the New King James Version of the Bible in your legal information. This not only protects you; it also lends a certain seriousness and credibility to your writing.

Documentation can appear within the context, as footnotes, as chapter endnotes, or as endnotes that all appear together in a special section at the end of the book, as seems fitting.

5.7 — What Is the Purpose of a Copyright Page?

A copyright page is a legal page, required by law, and it serves several purposes:

☐ **Identifying Your Rights:** The copyright page establishes your rights as the author of the book. The term *copyright* and the copyright symbol (©) protect you under American law, and the term ALL RIGHTS RESERVED protects you under international law.

☐ **Recognizing Other Sources:** The copyright page legally recognizes any other sources used in the book, in our case, especially Bible versions. When there are too many references from other books to cite on the copyright page, this can also be done in footnotes, chapter endnotes, book endnotes or another such special section.

□ **Establishing the ISBN:** The copyright page must list the ISBN (International Standard Book Number), the unique identifier of each book by which bookstores and distributors will recognize it, register it and sell it.

□ **Identifying the Publisher:** The copyright page identifies the publisher of the book and the publisher's contact information.

□ **Setting Forth Any Other Legal Information:** The copyright page holds any other legal information about the book, such as Library of Congress Cataloging Number (if applicable), country of printing, number of the current edition, etc. [19]

By law, the copyright page must be the first page following the title page.

---

19. Since, to obtain a Library of Congress Catalog Number, you must apply 6 months before publication of the book, and since most libraries do not handle Christian books, we have never found it convenient to use this feature.

5.8 — WHAT ARE ROYALTIES AND WILL YOU RECEIVE THEM?

Royalties are what is paid to an author when a publisher owns the rights to his or her book, publishes, promotes and sells the book, and then pays the author a small share of the profits. Usually that share is very small, less than ten cents per copy. Since, in our case, the author owns his own book, there are no royalties involved.

We do have, however, what is known as "sales forwarding." When someone else sells a book owned by the author, deducts a fair share of the sale price and forwards the rest of the payment to the publisher (to be forwarded to the author), that process is known in the book industry as "sales forwarding." So, instead of royalties, we have sales forwarding.

We do not keep a physical stock of any author's books. When we receive an order for your book through our web site, we forward that order to our printer for fulfillment. We then pay you for that sale, the same as any other retailer. Books are also sold by LSI and digital editions by other agencies.

When the agencies pay us, we forward 90% of the payment to the author, keeping 10% to help cover our expenses in managing the title, compiling and reporting the sales and forwarding payments. We report sales from all agencies (including our own sales) and disburse monies to our authors quarterly. Because LSI pays us 90 days after reporting the sales, our payments to the authors are one quarter behind the sales reports.

As noted elsewhere, we have partnered with Lightning Source International (LSI), a company that makes your book available to the largest booksellers in the world. If you missed that section, here's how it works. We register your book with LSI, setting the retail price and the wholesale discount. (Our normal bookstore discounts is 40%.) When LSI sells a book, they print the book, ship the book, and collect from the customer. Sales reports are sent to us monthly and at the end of 90 days, we receive payment for those sales. The amount forwarded to us is the difference between the sale price of the book and the cost of producing it. We then forward these funds to the respective authors, deducting 10% for our expenses. That is what we mean by sales forwarding.

5.9 — What Does a McDougal & Associates Publishing Contract Look Like?

A SAMPLE PUBLISHING CONTRACT

This contract will be between PUBLISHER, McDougal & Associates of 18896 Greenwell Springs Road, Greenwell Springs, LA 70739, and AUTHOR, <u>name and address</u>. Whereas AUTHOR has a book tentatively entitled <u>TITLE,</u> to be published and disseminated, the two parties hereby enter into the following contractual agreement concerning that book:

1. PUBLISHER and AUTHOR agree to a price of $1,099.00 (one thousand, nine hundred and ninety-nine dollars) for all setup costs (to be paid in full with the return of this signed contract). This setup fee will include:

    □ A professional editorial evaluation of the manuscript

- ☐ Professional typesetting
- ☐ A custom cover design based on the author's ideas, if any
- ☐ Complete copyright filing
- ☐ ISBN (International Standard Book Number) assignation and registration
- ☐ An EAN Barcode printed on the back cover
- ☐ Worldwide distribution from the McDougal & Associates website
- ☐ Placement in the ISBN database (making the book available to thousands of book retailers around the world)
- ☐ Placement of the book with the LSI POD system, making it available to Amazon. com, Barnes & Noble and many other online retailers and to the book distributors — Ingram Wholesale and Baker & Taylor — all for the purpose of wider dissemination
- ☐ Publishing and dissemination under the appropriate McDougal & Associates label
- ☐ Back cover text polishing
- ☐ An eBook option (some additional processing fees apply)
- ☐ A hardcover option (additional fees apply)

☐ On-demand printing (any number of copies at a time).

2. AUTHOR agrees to pay PUBLISHER an additional fee of (US$ <u>AMOUNT</u>) to edit the current manuscript, converting it into a more popular format, said fee to be paid as the work is completed to the author's satisfaction.

3. PUBLISHER agrees to upload the book to the LSI POD System and to order as many books as AUTHOR desires, and also to reorder books when desired. In each case, AUTHOR will pay only actual printing and shipping charges, plus a 10% surcharge over printer costs.

4. PUBLISHER agrees to pay AUTHOR, just like any other retailer, for any sales that come through its Internet site and 90% of all sales that come through the LSI System or other agencies (for digital editions), payments to be made quarterly.

5. Aside from these costs, no other charges will be made … unless (1) AUTHOR should decide to add too much additional material to the agreed-upon manuscript, (2) Too many last-minute changes are made, or (3) The book becomes larger than originally contracted.

6. Whenever AUTHOR decides to print additional books, the only charges that will be made above actual printing plus a 10% Publisher's Surcharge

and actual shipping of the books themselves will be changes to the text and or cover of the book required by AUTHOR. These will be billed to AUTHOR at a cost of $35.00 (thirty-five dollars) per hour. In addition, LSI, our printing partner, has a revision fee of $40 per revised file to be placed. This represents 1/2 hour of tech time at their going rate of $80 per hour.

_____   _____

Date

_____   _____

Signatures

"I'm so pleased that God led me to your publishing company. You did more than publish a book. You critiqued, edited, and helped in every way possible with the patience of Job. God bless you in this unique ministry He has given you.

Lowell Lytle
Pinellas Park, Florida
Author, *Diving into the Deep*

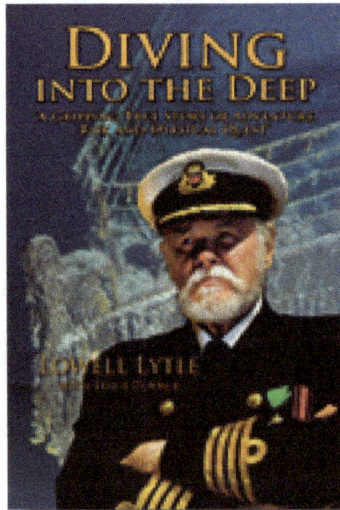

6. QUESTIONS ABOUT MARKETING YOUR BOOK

6.1 — What Have Others Done Before Us?

6.2 — How Can You Insure that You Have a Marketable Product to Sell?

6.3 — What Is Today's Challenge?

6.4 — What Can You Do Even Before Publication?

6.5 — What Can You Do During Publication?

6.6 — What Can You Do After Publication?

6.7 — What About Selling to Bookstores?

6.8 — How Can You Sell through Distributors?

6.9 — Should You Employ the Services of a Publicist?

6.10 — What Is the Conclusion on Marketing?

"I have been highly recommending McDougal & Associates to family and friends, and I will continue to do so. People are buying the book. The title and cover design catch their attention immediately, and then, when they open the book and see the layout, they love it. Thank you for that. There are other books that I must write, so you have not seen the last of me. To be continued."

Linda Gourdine-Hunt
Divine Inspirations Messenger
Springfield Gardens, New York
Author, *Help Wanted*
and *Good Evening, Heavenly Father, How Was Your Day?*

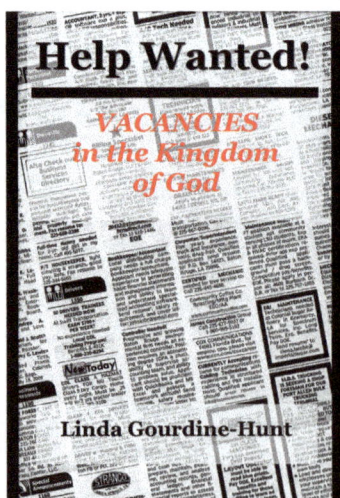

6.1 — WHAT HAVE OTHERS DONE BEFORE US?

Are you the first to encounter the problem of how to market your book? Hardly. You are among such great names as:

- ☐ William Blake
- ☐ Thomas Paine
- ☐ Robert Burns
- ☐ Walt Whitman
- ☐ Edgar Allen Poe
- ☐ Mark Twain (Samuel Clemons)
- ☐ Carl Sandburg
- ☐ James Joyce
- ☐ Washington Irving
- ☐ Ezra Pound
- ☐ Lord Byron

These are just a few of the many thousands of authors who have felt the need, through the years, of taking things into their own hands. For whatever reason, their early works were not picked up by the wealthy publishers of their day and promoted for them. Several of these authors didn't want to be controlled by secular publishers. They wanted more control over their work, sensing its importance. Others, perhaps, had no choice.

What about the publishing climate in our day? With the current intense competition in the marketplace, the insensitivity of the publishing industry to what God is saying to His people at the moment, and the overwhelming influence of profit as the major factor in publishing decisions today, many authors are resorting to doing it our way. And it works ... if you are willing to work at it.

There are some definite advantages to being your own promoter. For one, no one can do it quite like you can. You believe in your message, so you are its best promotor.

Here are some ideas that have worked for other authors. It can't hurt to give them a try. The important thing to remember is that you only need to sell the first copies of your book. After that, it will start selling itself.

6.2 — How Can You Insure that You Have a Marketable Product to Sell?

Marketing is an age-old art at which few people genuinely excel. We have all heard the old saying, "He is such a good salesman that he could sell refrigerators to the Eskimos." Some salesmen fit that description, but I doubt if there are many salesmen out there trying it. In order to sell enough refrigerators, a salesman would have to talk to a lot of Eskimos. Those Eskimos who are gullible enough to buy a refrigerator probably wouldn't dare recommend one to their friends and family members, and this is the greatest secret of marketing.

The salesman must sell the first examples of his product. From that point, the product should sell itself, that is, the product should be so good that those who buy it will recommend it to others. Word-of-mouth advertising always bears the greatest yield for your advertising dollar.

That brings up the question: do you have a quality product to promote? You may have a great message to present to the world or the Church, but if your book is not well written and well produced, no amount of marketing can make it successful.

Although marketing is important in our competitive world, the great bestsellers of our day do not attain that status through marketing alone. Their manuscripts must be properly edited and prepared to be worthy of proper promotion.

And not all bestselling authors are famous. Often very obscure individuals rise to fame because of the unmistakable quality of their books.

In the end, it is the individual reader who will judge the content and the author and make the book successful or unsuccessful. Will your book be recommended to neighbors and friends?

As you study the marketing strategies put forth here, please realize that we are assuming that the book you want to promote is a viable product. By that we mean that it has a good message, is well-written and interesting, is well-edited, is professionally typeset and printed and has an eye-catching title and cover design.

I have seen people who were so hungry for truth that they would read anything — literally. We have all heard, by now, of the hand-copied pages of Scripture so cherished by the people of the Eastern European countries during their time of severe persecution. It was all true. I have seen people thrilled by a roughly copied page. I have seen thousands grab for a tract printed on the cheapest newsprint. But that is all changing in our modern world. As the world gets more and more sophisticated and more and more material is available for people to read, poorly prepared materials simply don't stand a chance in this competitive atmosphere.

The same technology that has made it possible for more and more people to publish their materials has made it increasingly difficult to compete in the marketplace. With more than 20,000 new Christian titles making their way into the marketplace each year, you must have a quality product in order to compete successfully.

Publishing your book and successfully marketing it require that you first receive a proper critique of the book and a proper editing of the manuscript. Merely having a few friends or an English professor review your manuscript is no longer enough. A knowledge of the English language does not qualify one to critique or edit a book manuscript or determine its marketability.

Friends make poor critics of a manuscript for a couple of reasons:

□ They are so happy to have a friend who may soon become a published author that they rarely give an honest appraisal of the material.

- ☐ They are often afraid to hurt your feelings, so they don't dare to disagree with something you have said or criticize the way you have said it.

Therefore, you need to have your material reviewed by a third party, someone with no vested interests and nothing to lose, and whose primary interest is to make the book the best it can be, to give you some honest help with your manuscript.

The typesetting, cover design and then the actual manufacture of your book must all be done in a very professional way. A poorly designed and laid-out book will speak to those who see it of mediocrity and a lack of creativity.

The day of publishing typed pages or of using a poor quality printer for layout is past. Editors who work for the major publishers routinely throw away letters written on such printers. Even the quality of the letter speaks to them of an unprofessional approach that simply won't sell in today's marketplace.

Many Christian authors have friends who are budding artists or graphic designers and who offer to do the cover designs for their books. If the book is destined for a strictly local audience, this is all well and good. However, if your desire is to reach out to a larger audience, you will want to spend a little more and have something that you can be proud of and which will help to promote your book.

Whether we design your book, or whether you take it to some other professional publisher, you owe it to yourself to have it done according to national standards of quality. You may save a few hundred dollars by preparing everything yourself and taking it to a local printer. But, in the end, you will regret that decision. Your book will not have the proper format necessary to compete with other, similar books available in the market-place.

When a person buys your book and sits down in his easy chair with his cup of coffee or tea to read it, you don't want him to be distracted from the message of the book by the physical packaging. It is surprising how many things there are which can detract from the reader's enjoyment:

- ☐ The paper is not opaque and reflects too much light, straining the eyes.

- ☐ The paper was printed cross-grain, so the book is difficult open and keep open. In the industry, we call it "mouse-trapping."

- ☐ The book was trimmed out incorrectly.

- ☐ There are many grammatical errors.
- ☐ The thoughts do not flow well from one to another.
- ☐ Some statements could easily be misunderstood, leaving the reader confused.

The are just a few simple examples. There are many others. I wonder how many William Blakes, Thomas Paines, and Mark Twains there have been in recent history who have not been successful with their books simply because they failed to realize the importance of their proper preparation. Let us help you make your book all it can be.

6.3 — What Is Today's Challenge?

Promoting your own book can be both a challenging and rewarding experience. With God's help, thousand of believers are publishing their books each year, but when that book rolls off the press, the challenge has just begun. How to market it? That's the question.

God gives us a message, He shows us how to write it down effectively, and He shows us how to get it published, but how do we get it into the hands of the people who need it? What good is a ministry if it doesn't reach the people it was destined to help? What good is a gift if no one knows it exists? What good is a message if it is not disseminated? This is the challenge.

Authors are not usually marketing experts. They may know how to organize and express ideas, but many times they know absolutely nothing about how to market those ideas.

Sometimes the people we want to reach are sitting in church pews, and all we need do is secure a speaking engagement or advertise in the church bulletin or monthly magazine in order to let them know that help is available in the form of our books. But other people we want to reach may never go to church. They may be in bars or on street corners. How do we reach them?

Some Christian authors have advertised in newspapers such as *The National Enquirer*. The audience they hoped to reach, New Age adherents, read that scandal sheet. That is a very valid marketing strategy for Christians. Even Jesus walked among the publicans and sinners so He could lead them to Himself.

If the people we want to reach are found mostly in Bible schools, then we should contact Bible schools. If they are in sports circles, then we need to contact some sporting magazines and run ads in them. We need to use a variety of marketing techniques. But some Christians are hindered from using marketing, thinking that it is not only unspiritual, but even carnal.

When we think about it, however, marketing books is not unlike many other aspects of ministry. Someone must build the platform upon which an anointed evangelist will stand to minister to multitudes in a mass-evangelism crusade. Is the work of building the platform less spiritual than the work the evangelist will be doing? We may consider it so, but we're wrong.

If someone doesn't clean the church and make sure the heat is on during the winter, can the pastor effectively minister to his flock during service times? Adjusting the thermostat, sweeping the floor and teaching, then, are all equally important tasks.

What about the writing of the book? Was that all spiritual? Is there anything spiritual about making a pen mark on a piece of paper or pushing down the key of a computer keyboard? Aside from the revelation of the message itself, the process of writing the book contains many "unspiritual" aspects.

But without marketing, the message of your book will not reach its intended audience. The needy will not know that a book exists which can help them. The bills will not get paid, and you will not be able to go on writing and publishing more books. So, marketing is not beneath our dignity. It must be done.

Most of us haven't been very realistic about the sphere of influence we enjoy. It is very probable that the publishing of a book will increase our sphere of spiritual influence. There is not, however, any guarantee that all of us will become immediately known nationally or internationally, although this seems to be the expectation of many.

Most authors don't understand why a distributor cannot take their book and sell thousands of copies or why a Christian bookstore is reluctant to take more than a few copies at a time. Authors need to learn the realities of the marketing world.

We find that, at the beginning, most authors distribute their books successfully in their particular sphere of influence, whether small or great. Highly visible people can expect to distribute more books than others. That seems to leave a lot of us "out in the cold."

That is not necessarily the case. There are a number of very practical things any author can do to promote a book, and you don't need to be famous to do them. If we believe in the message we are promoting (enough to make an extra effort), we can expect, with time, to achieve the desired results.

6.4 — What Can We Do Even Before Publication?

Much interest can be stirred up about your book even as it is going through the publication process. You can actually begin as soon as you have made the determination to publish. There are a number of effective ways of promoting your book before you have it in your hand. Here are a few suggestions that other authors have found helpful:

Announcement Letters

Prepare a pre-publication announcement letter and send it out to everyone on your mailing list. If you don't have a mailing list, you may be able to request that the letter be sent to those on your church's mailing list. If it goes out with some other church mailing, you could offer to share the cost of the mailing. If your letter goes out alone, you will probably have to pay the entire mailing cost. Our busy society is still doing a lot of its shopping by mail, and mail-order houses of all types abound, testimony that this is still an effective marketing strategy. If you are communicating on a regular basis through email, a blog, use of social media or texting on your smart phone, then, by all means, use that media to communicate about your book.

Much of the success or failure of such a mailing will depend largely on the content and layout of the announcement letter itself. While preparing it, remember that people are busy and that they get a lot of "junk" mail, so you must make your impact quickly. The letter should be short, to the point, well spaced on the paper for visual impact, and well written to convey the message you desire.

Address the needs of those to whom you are writing:

☐ What is special about this book?

☐ Why do those receiving the letter need it?

☐ What will it do for them?

Include a brief one- or two-paragraph synopsis of the book and perhaps a few of the chapter titles. To make it easy for readers to order the book, include a simple order form with the letter. For those who shop online, include a web link. In any case, you should offer a discount to those who order the book in advance.

ADS IN PERIODICALS

A pre-publication ad for your book could be contained in a periodical (either printed or online) that will go out to the target audience. If your church or group has such a publication, explore the possibility of advertising in it. Such ads are, of necessity, small (contact the periodical for complete details about size specifications). It must, therefore, make an impact with few words.

Use your brief synopsis of the book with, perhaps, a few of the chapter titles to create interest. Include the book title in bold letters and a prominent "kicker," such as, "COMING SOON!" or "SOON TO BE RELEASED!" Since recent generations are graphic oriented, begin to include a good quality graphic of the book cover as soon as it becomes available.

BULLETIN INSERTS

The announcement letter, a copy of the ad, or a specially prepared page can be used as a bulletin insert in local churches that know and trust you. This has proven to be a very effective means of marketing Christian books.

Follow many of the same guidelines for preparing the insert as for the letter or ad. One possibility is to use both sides of the paper and put an order form on the back.

Another effective idea is to make your bulletin insert in the form of a bookmark that people will keep in their Bibles or important books. Such a bookmark will serve as a constant reminder.

Avoid the use of poor quality photocopy in all your promotional materials. If your advertisement looks amateurish, potential buyers will feel that your book is probably amateurish as well. Let the promotional piece reflect the same high standard of quality as the book itself.

UTILIZING SOCIAL MEDIA

Today many are using the social media as a means of promoting all sorts of things. Some have set up a special Facebook page for their book or ministry or both. Some are placing ads on Facebook and other social media sites and being very successful with it. This makes sense. If you are contacting people who love you or love your message through the use of these social media, then that is a logical place to let people know that your book will soon be available and how they can get it.

SETTING UP YOUR OWN WEBSITE

Although your book will appear on many websites as part of the POD print system (our own site ThePublishedWord.com, as well as Amazon.com, BN.com, and many others that take their feed from

Amazon), some have chosen to set up a special site just for their book. If you already have a ministry site or a personal site, then that's the place to advertise and promote your book. If not, you may want a site just for the book itself.

In former years, building and maintaining a web site was a task for a professional, and so it was rather expensive for the average person. Now, however, prices have come way down, and web building software has improved and been simplified to the point that most everyone can operate it (if you're willing to take the time to learn). In this way, you can make changes or additions to the site yourself. Since young people grow up doing these things, if you are of the older generations, you might want to ask someone in your family to do it for you.

Having the software necessary to process credit cards is more expensive than just maintaining a web site. After exploring prices, you can decide if you wish to actually process the orders yourself, or if you would rather send them to another site and let someone else handle that part of the process. Creating a link to another site is relative easy.

6.5 — WHAT CAN YOU DO DURING PUBLICATION?

The artwork for the cover of your book is usually completed a few weeks in advance of the finished book. You can use that cover design to good advantage. Having an actual cover in your hand adds life to the book. It proves that this is no longer just a possibility; it is a reality. Now, repeat the process.

REPEAT THE PROCESS

At this point, the announcement letter, the ads in periodicals and bulletin inserts can be repeated, adding a reduced copy of the cover of the book. Many people don't order a book the first time they read about it. They may be interested, but they're thinking that there's still plenty of time. The second mention often catches the procrastinators. Be sure the front cover of the book is prepared properly if you use black and white printing on your advertising piece. A sharp cover, even in black and white, will help to sell your book.

If you use a mailing list, make a small note at the bottom of the letter, "If you have already placed your order, please ignore this reminder" to avoid offending those who have already ordered. Or, remove the names of those who have already ordered from the list of those who will receive this piece.

You will want to keep a list of all those who buy your book. If and when you publish another book, you will have a good pool of prospective customers.

There are now some other things you can do:

OTHER SPECIAL MAILINGS

For a small fee, we can provide you with a PDF file of the book cover that you can take to a local quick print and have them run off a few hundred copies on a more flexible stock for promotional use. These make excellent advertising tools. We suggest that you use them for a special mailing to the following:

- ☐ **KEY LEADERS:** Key leaders often have spiritual influence over large groups of people. If they feel that your book is worthy, they might do much to promote it, even using it in their own ministries.

- ☐ **PASTORAL GROUPS:** The same is true of pastoral groups. Pastors are looking for good material to use for study groups or to recommend to people they counsel. Helping them to get to know your book doesn't guarantee you sales, but it certainly can't do any harm.

☐ **TELEVISION AND RADIO PROGRAM HOSTS:** Radio and TV programs are looking for fresh faces to interview concerning current topics of interest. If your book falls into this category, you might expect a number of invitations. Don't be hesitant to express to the potential interviewer your need to promote the book, not just talk about its content. If you have success in this area on a local level, build on that success to gain a more regional opportunity, contacting stations in larger cities. When you do, always refer to the interviews you've already had on local stations.

☐ **CONFERENCE CENTERS:** People who attend conferences on a regular basis are some of the most spiritually hungry people in our society. They are always looking for good books. Aside from your own church and its regular contacts, you might want to contact businessmen's fellowships and similar ladies and young people's groups. Every year people flock to summer camps, expecting new things from God. Especially in the South, there are many of these camps where you might gain exposure for your ministry and your book.

PRESS RELEASES

Newspapers usually find it very interesting when a local author is about to publish a book. Send a simple press release. In your accompanying letter, state that you would be happy to do an interview, if requested.

REGULAR CORRESPONDENCE

If you are like many other authors, you have a lot of personal correspondence. Take advantage of this fact by enclosing a promotional piece with every letter you send out. Don't take it for granted that all your regular correspondents know about the book, and don't worry about a few repetitions over a period of weeks. This is a normal advertising tactic.

A SPECIAL PAMPHLET

Since you are an author and have researched and written on a certain subject, your opinions of this subject are respected. Try writing a pamphlet on the subject and distributing it free of charge as a ministry. At the end of the message, you can advertise your book. The pamphlet will serve to get people's interest. It will catch the attention of those who will read short stories or articles, but who wouldn't normally pick up a book. Large publishers use this strategy, usually taking interesting excerpts from the book as the material for the pamphlet. These brochures can be added to convention packets, used as bulletin inserts, or sent as part of press releases to selected newspapers.

The press release may announce the availability of the free pamphlet for those who write. Readers are directed to send a self-addressed, stamped envelope. This is a low-cost way of getting information about your book into the hands of the people who need it. If using the more modern media, encourage readers to leave their email address or to respond to a social media posting.

Now that more and more people are reading online, prepare all of your notices as emails and web articles that can be circulated, always including a link to your main sales site.

6.6 — What Can You Do After Publication?

Once you have the physical book in your hand, quickly mail out copies that have been pre-ordered. The book is the best advertisement you can use. You might enclose a note with the books that go out, thanking those who ordered in advance and telling them how to order additional copies and quoting volume prices.

Now the serious work of marketing begins. The theme of your advertising now changes from "SOON TO BE RELEASED" to "NEWLY RELEASED," "RECENTLY RELEASED," or something similar.

At this point, the announcement letter, the ads in periodicals, the bulletin inserts, the special mailings, the press releases, the newspaper, radio and television interviews, the regular correspondence, the use of the special pamphlet, the social media outlets and web site contacts should be repeated — emphasizing that the book is now available. Those who have put off ordering may now act.

Aside from these, there are additional measures that you should take:

SENDING OUT COMPLIMENTARY COPIES

Since the book is the very best piece of advertising you could use, send complimentary copies to the following:

☐ People who have shown more than a casual interest in the book

☐ People who have a similar burden to that expressed in the book

☐ People who have the necessary influence to help promote the book

These will include many of those we have already mentioned: the key leaders, the pastoral groups, the radio and television program hosts, and the conference center leaders. But there are other possibilities. For instance, offer to send two copies of the book to local Christian radio and television stations for review, along with information about yourself. Radio and television stations often use books as promotional items and might be interested in purchasing your book in volume. Consider giving the station a good discount (we suggest 50% to 60% if possible). Bless them, and they will be more likely to help you.

Send at least one copy of the book to several major national ministries. Begin with those who seem to be saying the same thing you are saying in the book, those you like particularly and would trust to distribute your book. Often, we especially like a certain ministry because we are of kindred spirits. Again, offer a good discount on the book. National ministries have a large overhead, which they constantly need to meet.

Send copies to Christian magazines and periodicals for review. If they do a review of your book, that's free advertising. Those in which you place your own ads should be the logical first targets, but consider others.

Some magazines don't have a book review section, but they do have a book announcement section. Follow the instructions of the particular periodical for preparing the required ad copy.

Local Christian and civic organizations are often looking for good speakers. They are pleased that a local personality has published a book and will invite you to speak. Offer to send a free copy of the book to the organization's officers. If you are invited to speak, you can put a plug in for your book during the talk.

OTHER SPEAKING ENGAGEMENTS

As Christians, the normal outlet of our ministry is through churches, youth groups, conferences, camps meetings, etc. Speaking engagements in these places can often be the greatest outlet for our books. When people hear us minister, they want to get our books so they can learn more.

Many of those who organize these activities and who are constantly looking for special speakers will not know that you are available. For many of us, it is not "in character" to promote ourselves as special speakers. Yet this is the way it is done.

Send a letter to those who organize such activities, mentioning the book and your availability to speak on the same or related subjects. Provide a phone number and email address where you can be reached, since most of these people are busy and do their scheduling either by phone or email. When they call or write, have your calendar ready so that you can accept or decline an invitation.

BOOK PARTIES

Parties are thrown for everything these days: Tupperware parties, Amway parties, even lingerie parties. Why should we shrink from using this very popular and effective means of marketing for our books?

Ask some good friends or family members to use their house as a gathering place. Let them invite their family members, neighbors and friends.

Serve some refreshments. Then tell them about your book, how you received the message from the Lord, and how the publication came about. Discuss the major thrust of the book and what it will do for those who read it.

Solicit the help of those who attend the book party in promoting the book and put some type of promotional material into their hands (a pamphlet, for example). Offer to sign the book personally for anyone who would like it. Close by sending everyone to the book table to buy. Have information on volume discounts available in case anyone shows interest in purchasing multiple copies.

If you have close friends in other cities, they might want to organize such a party. You could use the opportunity to minister to their neighbors and friends. Many people will come to such events when they won't go to church.

BOOK SIGNINGS

A modern term for a book party may be a book signing. Organize or have someone else organize it for you, and do all of the things mentioned above. For a fair share of the profit, local Christian bookstores will do book signings for you, but it is best for you to provide them the needed books on consignment.

SMALL CHRISTIAN NEWSPAPERS

Church groups and/or small publishers often have a magazine in which ads of all types can be placed. Learn what is available in your community and others, the costs involved and how to take advantage of it. Those who read these newspapers are often pastors and other church leaders, heads of ministries, owners or operators of Christian bookstores and other interested individuals.

CREATE AN AUTHOR INFORMATION PAGE ON AMAZON.COM

Amazon.com allows each author to create an author information page. This can be very helpful when your titles pop up for reader's to view. Don't be too bashful to prepares such a page or to ask someone to do it for you.

6.7 — What About Selling to Bookstores?

With your book in the POD system, you are covered as far as bookstores are concerned. However, making the book available does not guarantee it sales. You must do some promotion for it.

If you intend to hold special meetings in a certain town, notify the bookstore/s there in advance so that they can have some of your book/s on hand. Since most bookstore depend on being able to return any books that don't sell and we allow no returns, offer to place some books with them on consignment, always being aware that they need a good discount to make it worth their while.

Please consider: with the large number of Christian books now on the market, bookstores face a terrible dilemma. It is literally impossible for them to carry every available book in stock. Most bookstores can't even afford to carry every Bible available, let alone every book. The books that sell well for them (and help them pay the bills) are well-advertised books on timely subjects by well-known authors.

This doesn't mean that your book can't sell in bookstores. It just means that you may have to make an extra effort to see that they do. When we place you in the LSI system, your book automatically becomes available to every bookstore in America. But will they buy it? They will need a compelling reason to do so.

If there is a Christian bookstore in your area, begin with that one. Call or, if possible, visit the purchasing agent and talk to him about your book. If you have invitations to do some radio or television interviews, you will be interviewed in a local newspaper, or will be speaking in some local churches, the bookstore owners may see that it's to their advantage to carry your book.

Many bookstores may be reluctant to carry your book unless they have a larger-than-usual discount on it or are selling them on consignment. The standard bookstore discount is 40%. That may seem like a lot to some authors. You must remember, however, that the bookstore owner has to pay rent, salaries, utilities, insurance and advertising. He needs a good discount in order to exist.

Some authors are offended when a bookstore owner orders five copies. This is probably the average purchase per title. If you are doing enough promotion in the neighborhood, more will be sold. Let the owner know that he can order through

Ingram Wholesale, but that, unfortunately, we cannot afford to provide bookstores with the possibility to return the books they order. That may discourage some, but believe me, you can't afford returns.

Pass by that store occasionally to see how sales are progressing and give them a little pep talk. Sometimes local bookstores have ideas for promotions that you can do together. For example, you can advertise on radio, television and newspaper that you will be present in the store for a signing on a specific day. They love that. Perhaps you can share the cost of special posters to be placed in the store and in churches, advertising the book and the store. Ask the storeowner for other ideas.

If you agree to leave books on consignment with a store, keep good records, and remember whom you spoke with. With many staff members coming and going, it can get confusing.

Another place you might explore the possibility of selling through bookstores is in any area where you regularly minister and are known. All the same things hold true in these cases.

Aside from Christian bookstores, other types of stores often carry books and magazines. Local grocery stores, convenience stores, and newspaper stands sometimes would be happy to carry your book by the cash register if you are known locally. Consider offering these stores a greater-than-bookstore discount. Again, you may want to put the books there on consignment (if the vendor requires it). If nothing sells, you have lost nothing. You have to try. Those who make the necessary effort sell books.

6.8 – How Can You Get Your Books into the Hands of Distributors?

The New

Fortunately, with your book in the LSI Print-On-Demand system, this is taken care of for you. The corporate owner of LSI, Ingram Books, is the largest distributor of Christian books in the world. Your books will also be available through the industry giant Baker & Taylor. So rest assured that you are taken care of with distributors. The discount you are offering to bookstores (typically 40%) will cover distributors as well.

The Old

Before the days of this wonderful system we had to advise our authors as follows:

There are several national and international distributors whose ministry is getting your books into the hands of the people who want and need them. These professionals deal with many thousands of titles, so their job is not easy. There are some things you can do to encourage them to take your book for distribution.

Begin advising distributors about your book before publication. In your letter, mention the title, the theme, something about yourself (but not your entire life's story), your mailing address and phone number, the retail price of the book and the discount you offer.

The standard distributor's discount is 55%. Many need more. Don't be scandalized by that. Consider that the distributor will give the bookstore a minimum of 40% discount, that the distributor also has expenses and that he needs to show a small profit. They're not cheating you. Marketing costs money.

Any number of things might encourage the distributor to take your book. If you already have been or will soon be exposed to the public through radio or television programs or through some form of magazine or newspaper article, tell the distributor about it.

Many people have a built-in market. (By that I mean that they are known and appreciated in certain circles, where their books will automatically sell well.) If that is your case, let the distributor know that. Tell the distributor any other facts that will give him confidence that the purchase of your books will result in sales.

When you think sufficient time has passed after your first letter (about two or three weeks), give the distributor a call to ask if they got the letter and whether they have considered the book. Don't be surprised if they are non-committal. Ask if they would like to receive a complimentary copy when the book is published. Be persistent. It may take several phone calls to get the attention you need. These are busy people.

When the cover is ready, repeat the process to those you feel are interested, this time enclosing the cover.

If distributors are still hesitant, you may need to offer a larger discount or to send them the books on consignment. It can get complicated, but these are the realities of the marketplace.

Keep a record on the people you deal with at the distributorship and ask for them personally when you call. Keep good records of how many books you send and on what basis. People forget and sometimes need to be reminded. If you have no record, you may also forget.

THE CONCLUSION

You can forget the old and embrace the new because you will be in the system. We must caution our authors, however, that even though your book is in the POD system, there is no guarantee that it will sell — through bookstores, through dis-tributors or through online retailers. Unless you somehow create some interest in your book and people know it exists, no one will go into a brick and mortar bookstore or an online bookstore and ask for it. You, as the author, need to create that interest.

6.9 — Should You Employ the Services of a Publicist?

What is a publicist? According to Wikipedia, the online dictionary, "A publicist is a person whose job it is to generate and manage publicity for a public figure, especially a celebrity, a business, or for a work such as a book, film or album. Most top-level publicists work in private practice, handling multiple clients." [20] Publicists can be hired to promote a book.

What might a publicist do for you? For instance, they might get you radio or television interviews, and the interest those interviews generate could create more sales for your book. Why, then, is there any question?

☐ Most publicists don't work cheap. The simplest package they offer, usually consisting of radio interviews you do by telephone from your home, will cost you several thousand dollars. Television interviews are even more expensive, and print media costs go on up the ladder.

20. www.en.wikipedia.org/wiki/Publicist

□ Our experience with publicists has not been a productive one. In a former time many Christian radio and television stations were looking for good interviews and even did them free. Today, most Christian talk radio has given way to the more popular easy-listening music, so those still doing interviews are generally not Christian and are looking for a secular emphasis.

If you can afford a publicist, then find a good one. Most of us can neither afford nor benefit from their services.

6.10 — What Is the Conclusion on Marketing?

So what is the conclusion of all of this: As a self-publisher, you are not without marketing tools. There is much that you can do. In the final analysis, however, no distributor or bookstore can guarantee the sale of your book. No catalog, no direct mailing effort can guarantee that it will reach its desired audience. It is the consumer who finally decides, by buying or not buying your book, whether it is financially successful or not.

With the odds stacked against you because of the proliferation of well-advertised books by well-known authors banging into each other in the marketplace, you need two key elements to help you find the desired market:

☐ You need patience.

☐ You need prayer.

It may take time for you to be known as an author and for people to want your books. It doesn't always happen with one interview or one ad or one letter. It takes a consistent effort over a period of time.

If your share of the market at first seems to be largely localized, realize that this is not unusual. Making your work known regionally, nationally, and internationally takes more time. Don't be discouraged if you don't gain the recognition you desire overnight.

If you have a localized market, thank God for a market. It's better to have a localized market than no market at all. If you try to promote your book beyond the borders of your current outreach, you may simply exhaust your financial resources and bring your publishing ministry to an end. Don't risk that. Let it grow naturally.

You may be influential in only one region or in several isolated regions. Be happy for your influence in those regions and allow the Spirit of God to expand you into other areas.

Where does God want these materials distributed? If He gave you the message, helped you to put it together into a book (a phenomenal task), and helped you to get it published, He can help you to market it successfully. Seek His face concerning every aspect of marketing. Ask Him to give you wisdom about who and when and how and where. He is faithful and will show you strategies that even we may never have heard of.

As your ministry grows, let all your published materials promote each other. Mention the books you have published on the CDs you send out. Take a special page or two at the back of the next book you produce to advertise the availability of your CD albums and any other ministry tools you may have, including other book titles.

You might include loose inserts in all the books you mail out, advertising other items. [21]

If your book seems to be attracting more than casual interest, consider submitting it for publication by a major national publisher. It can happen, and you have nothing to lose by trying.

There are several ways to choose a publisher for the submission of a manuscript. If you like a particular line of books or you see books that are related to your theme, that might give you a place to begin. Write a letter, noting the success your book has enjoyed and inviting comment. You might be pleasantly surprised by the response.

Some Christian authors have found that their writing skills gave them an open door to write as a regular columnist for rural or small newspapers. Sometimes they were even able to use excerpts from their book/s as material for the column. One column may lead to another. Don't limit God.

Finally, how do you measure success? The definition of success varies a lot from individual to

21. Such inserts are not permitted in books sold through distributors.

individual. For many, success is measured only by the bottom line. Have enough books been sold to require a reprint? Is the profit margin acceptable? These considerations are not unimportant, especially if you have other books you want to publish.

Others have a very different view of success. If they can just sell enough books to cover the initial costs involved in the project, they are happy. Some are not concerned at all with the bottom line. Just the fact that they have been obedient to God in preparing and publishing His message is enough for them. They leave the rest in His hands.

Some gauge the success of the book by the number of people to whom it ministers. If, as a result of the book, lives are changed, marriages are mended, or church life improves, who cares about the bottom line?

Others feel successful because of the many new contacts they have made through the book. They may not have a great profit margin, but many doors of ministry have opened to them, and they feel fulfilled in that way.

Each person must be satisfied in his own heart that he has done what he was intended to do and that the methods he has used to promote his book or books are those that the Lord indicated.

7. QUESTIONS ABOUT THE NEW WORLD OF eBOOKS

"Words escape me when I attempt to convey the quality of work and the valuable asset I have found in McDougal & Associates. I received a small company's personal service but came away with a large company's quality end product. They included me in every step of the process in perfecting my book for its eventual publication. To have others treat my work with dignity was, in itself, a great source of validation."

Rita Anderson
Ponchatoula, Louisiana
Author, *Poetic Ponderings and Piths*

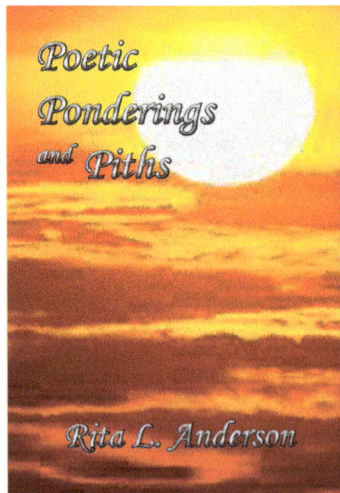

7.1 — INTRODUCTION TO eBOOKS

In recent years, the growth in sales of eBooks has begun to outpace, for the first time, the growth in sales of printed editions. As more and more companies produce better, smaller and less expensive digital readers, and as more and more books become available in the digital formats, this growth promises to keep exploding exponentially. This is a whole new world, and you will want to take advantage of it to get your message out.

7.2 — WHAT ARE eBOOKS AND HOW ARE THEY PRODUCED?

The term *eBook* simply means "electronic book." An eBook or electronic book is actually nothing more than a digital file that can be read on a variety of eBook readers. [22]

Here's what Wikipedia, the online dictionary, has to say about eBooks:

> An electronic book (variously: e-book, eBook, e-Book, ebook, digital book, or even e-edition) is a book-length publication in digital form, consisting of text, images, or both, readable on computers or other electronic devices. Although sometimes defined as "an electronic version of a printed book," many e-books exist without any printed equivalent. Commercially produced and sold e-books are usually intended to be read on dedicated e-book readers, however, almost any sophisticated electronic device that features a controllable viewing screen, including computers, many mobile phones, and all smartphones can also be used to read e-books. [23]

---

22. For more details on eBook readers, see the following section
23. http://en.wikipedia.org/wiki/E-book

The first practical modern eBooks were a result of the Adobe adoption of the portable file format (PDF). PDFs could be easily created, easily attached to emails, easily downloaded, and easily viewed by others. They quickly became the industry standard for sharing and viewing documents online. Since Adobe Reader was a free program, it was downloaded onto millions of computers around the world, and millions of readers suddenly had the ability to download and view eBooks in this exciting format.

Since Adobe software has been the printing industry standard for many years now, this was convenient for publishers, since they now had the software to produce PDFs from most any other document, including book layouts.

But the Adobe Reader format has its limitations. It is what is called a "fixed format." This simply means that a PDF eBook page looks exactly like the printed page it was generated from. The only difference is that it can be transported and then viewed at any size. As the page view percentage is reduced, however, what you see on the screen is also reduced proportionally, for it is "fixed."

In the meantime, many others utilized the growing power of computers and the Internet to painstakingly type in public documents and then books that were already in the public domain.

These usually appeared as HTML files and reading them was limited to those who had access to computers. They were stored on the Internet and also on CDs (even floppy disks at first).

Sensing the potential to change the way the world reads, many companies jumped on the eReader bandwagon and began developing and producing readers of their own. This quickly produced many very different and very incompatible formats, and readers were discouraged by not knowing which technology would prevail in the end.

In the late 1990s, it was agreed that a standard for eBook development was needed, and several large companies joined forces to develop that standard. Together they formed the International Digital Publishing Forum (IDPF) and began working on eBook standards.

What the IDPF came up with was a variation on HTML that utilizes a system known as CSS (Cascading Style Sheets) to tell a digital reading device how to format the text on the screen. The resulting Files is called an EPUB.

Wikipedia describes the IDPF and the EPUB format it developed in this way:

The International Digital Publishing Forum (IDPF) is a trade and standards association for the digital publishing industry, that has been set up in order to establish a reliable and complete standard for ebook publishing. This is the organization responsible for the EPUB standard currently used by most e-readers.

Starting from the Open eBook Publication Structure or "OEB" (1999), which was created loosely around HTML, it then defined the OPS (Open Publication Structure), the OPF (Open Packaging Format) and the OCF (Open Container Format). These formats are the basis for the common EPUB and Mobipocket [24] ebook file formats. [25]

EPUB stands for "Electronic Publication." This type of file is known in the industry as "free-flowing" or "reflowable." What this means is that nothing is fixed. The text moves to fill the monitor it is being viewed on. This is necessary, for instance, not only because computer monitors come in all sizes, but because books are now being viewed on iPads, Kindle and Nook (and comparable) readers of various sizes, and even smartphones.

Until recently, most digital reading devices had their own built-in fonts and did not recognize or utilize any fonts listed in the book file. Also most readers were black and white. As color was introduced, more fonts or embedded fonts were

24. Mobipocket refers to the format adopted by Amazon and now known as Kindle.
25. http://en.wikipedia.org/wiki/International_Digital_Publishing_Forum. "

supported, and graphic elements could be viewed with ease, everything changed. In fact, the requirements for creating EPUB files are constantly changing.

After the formation of the International Digital Publishing Forum and their decision to standardize eBook formatting, Amazon, which had already captured 80% of online print book sales, made the startling decision to buy a company called Mobipocket and utilize its MOBI technology for its own eBooks (now known as Kindle) rather than accept the EPUB standard. MOBI files are similar to EPUB files, but they use their own formatting. Therefore, when we prepare our Kindle editions, we must add the extra step that converts an EPUB into the acceptable Kindle format.

A given book looks different on every reader, so it is no longer possible to insist on our own look. That is pretty much out of our hands.

As to how such files are produced, some specialty software has been developed that aids those who work with EPUBs every day, but as before, Adobe has maintained itself at the forefront of the publishing industry, so the same software we use to typeset books can also be utilized to produce EPUB files.

7.3 — What Is Needed To Read an eBook?

An eBook can be read on any computer that supports reading software, such as Adobe Digital Editions (which, I understand, is intended to eventually replace the long-standard Adobe Reader). Other free reading software includes Kindle for PC and Calibre. But increasingly eBooks are being read on a dedicated reader, such as Nook or Kindle. As the quality of these and other readers increases and the price of them falls, more and more people are buying them and beginning their eBook adventures.

eBooks are also read on tablets like iPad and its Android cousins and on smartphones — including Apple, Android and Windows editions.

Some readers can handle a variety of formats. Most of them can handle standard EPUBs.

7.4 — WHO DISTRIBUTES EBOOKS?

We offer all of our various eBooks from our site, but most eReaders (digital reading devices) are designed to download books from a particular site, so each agency distributes their own format:

- ☐ **KINDLE:** Amazon distributes Kindle books, so we register our Kindle titles with them, uploading a copy of the proper file, and they distribute it and report to us monthly on sales. Kindle bookstores have now been opened in many countries other than the US.

- ☐ **NOOK:** Barnes and Noble distributes Nook books, so we upload our Nook versions to them, and they report to us monthly on sales. Nook stores have now been opened in many countries other than the US.

- ☐ **iBOOK:** Apple distributes iBooks on its iTune site. We are blessed, however, in that LSI, our printing partner, is an authorized aggregator for iTunes. We upload our iBook versions to the LSI site, and they take charge of seeing that they get to iTunes and then report to us monthly on sales.

☐ **ADOBE DIGITAL EDITIONS:** Again, we are blessed in that LSI, our printing partner, has a digital division that makes Adobe Digital Editions books available to many other online retailers. We upload our PDF eBooks to them, and they report to us monthly on sales.

Here is a list of the resellers who currently draw their feed from LSI:

IN THE U.S. AND CANADA

Better World Books, Cokesbury.com, Complete-book.com, Covenant, DMC, eBookMall, Hastings, Kobo Books, Lybrary.com, Majesty Media Group, Mardel Inc., Mediander LLC, Parable, Premier Digital Publishing, Slikebooks, Spoiled Milk, WOWIO, and XAMonline.

IN EUROPE

BOL.com, Bookshop Krisostomus, eBook.de, eCommSource, Feedbooks, LaFeltrinelli.com, www. riider.com, tookbook.com, Tradebit, txtr.com, UAB VIPsupply, and Webster.

In Other Countries

Asia Books (Thailand), Booktopia (Australia) Disal, livriasaraiva.com.br and SBS.com.br (Brasil), eBook-Shop and Kalahari.net (South Africa), Infibeam, Online Book and Place (India), MPH Online (Malaysia).

7.5 — How Are eBooks Priced?

Most, but not all, eBooks are priced very reasonably. Apple requires, for example, that all iBooks be priced below $10, and they must end in .99. The lowest price would be .99, then 1.99, 2.99, 3.99, etc. Our custom until now has been to place a retail price of about half what the printed version of the book sells for. Some opt for a lower retail price, and some opt for going higher. One author in particular asked to have his digital editions reduced to $3.99, but his sales did not increase appreciably. Another author raised the price of his eBooks, and his sales increased. So pricing isn't a science.

As a general rule, we want to price books at a happy medium. As this industry continues to change, the price of eBooks may fall, but the volume should rise to counter that expected loss. The good news is that you can earn as much or more selling an eBook as you can selling a printed version. (See the following section.)

7.6 — WHAT WOULD YOU EARN ON THE SALE OF AN eBOOK?

Surprisingly, you can actually earn more from the sale of eBooks than you can from the sale of the same book in printed form. The reason is that the reseller discount is much lower with eBooks:

☐ **Kindle**: In some cases (for sales within the U.S.), Amazon will pay 70% of the sale to the author. For sales outside the U.S., the royalty falls to 30%. It can fall even further for special promotions.

☐ **Nook**: Barnes and Noble pays 40%.

☐ **iBook**: Apple pays 64%.

☐ **Adobe Digital Editions**: With LSI, we set the discount, and we usually make it only 25%, so the author receives 75% of the sale.

All of these agencies report sales monthly, but some take 90 days to pay afterward, so we report and disburse funds quarterly, and payments are always one quarter behind reported sales. As with print editions, McDougal & Associates deducts 10% from sales before forwarding the balance to authors.

7.6 — What eBook Formats Does McDougal & Associates Produce?

We have the software to produce fifteen different formats, but many of these have a limited following. We, therefore, produce and sell eBooks in the four most popular formats:

- Kindle
- Nook
- Apple iBook [26]
- Adobe Digital Editions

---

26. The Nook and iBook formats are actually very much the same. To customize the books, we prepare a different copyright page for each of these, and then they are uploaded to different agencies.

7.8 — What Would It Cost To Have Your Book Done in the Digital Formats?

This cost has come down dramatically. If we have your files already typeset for the print version, we can then reconfigure those files and use them to process the digital editions. The costs are as follows:

- □ $75 for the first digital edition
- □ $50 for each additional digital edition
- □ $39 for the one unique ISBN required

If we must first drop your material into a typesetting template or bring it up to standard from an older typeset format before generating the digital editions, the charge for that extra work is $250.

7.9 — What Are the Differences Between the Layout of the Print Version and the Digital Editions?

The differences between typesetting a book for print and for digital editions are dramatic:

□ Many of the fonts used for years in printing will not work in digital editions. For this reason, Adobe has developed all new fonts, known as Open Type fonts, for this purpose. Some digital readers still only utilize their internal, built-in fonts and do not recognize the fonts used in or embedded in the eBook layout. For this reason, we have much less control over the look of an eBook than we have over the look of its printed cousin.

□ All vertical spacing is lost in digital editions. I suppose this is to conserve space. As a publisher, it is aggravating, but that's the reality.

- ☐ All empty pages are omitted in digital editions. They would serve no practical purpose.

- ☐ Any and all graphics used in digital editions must appear "inline" with the text that precedes and follows them. They cannot be placed independently as they were before.

- ☐ The Graphic elements used in eBooks cannot be of the same high resolution required for books in print.

- ☐ All text intended to be kept together must be placed in order.

- ☐ Any material you wish to have on a separate page must be placed in a separate document. These separate documents are then linked in what is known as a book file. [27]

Now that we know these quirks and are doing more and more digital editions of our books, we plan for them from the start of each project, and much extra work is eliminated.

---

27. Recent alternatives have been developed that can omit this step.

7.10 — What Is the Difference Between Fixed-Page and Free-Flowing eBooks?

There are two basic types of digital format: fixed-page and free-flowing. Adobe Reader utilizes the fixed-page format. Whatever your print page looks like, your digital version will look exactly the same, although perhaps larger or smaller. Depending on the size of the monitor on which the page is viewed, the fixed-page format requires that the viewer change page views to see some items.

With the free-flowing format used by the majority of newer digital reading devices, the text and graphics move to fit whatever space is available on the screen. This is what makes possible viewing a book page on an iPhone. Because authors (and publishers) have worked hard to maintain a certain look to their pages, it can be disconcerting to see everything change to fit the screen being used.

Instructions for creating eBooks state that a publisher should test the finished product on every possible device to make sure it works well on each one. With the proliferation of available devices now on the market, this is nearly impossible. So far, however, we have had no complaints about our eBooks not working properly.

7-11— eBook Standards Keep Evolving

Electronic books are still so new to the market that they are always evolving, and the standards for them are constantly being updated. This has a lot to do with the capabilities of the latest batch of digital readers. It is not unusual to receive a new directive every few months as to resolution, fonts used, graphics, etc., and it is a lot to keep up with. Fortunately, since we use the most cutting edge software on the market, we can stay abreast of these changes and continue to improve the quality and also the affordability of our eBooks.

8. QUESTIONS ABOUT MCDOUGAL & ASSOCIATES

"People who see the book take a long hard look at the cover and like it, and that helps me as I begin to share with them a little about the title and subtitle. Many really like the pulled words, and I do too! I'm soooo glad you made that addition. Everyone comments on the simple way the book is written. They like that. This evening a gal that just received the book said that she was using it as a devotional. Another comment I hear a lot is: 'It's like someone sitting in my living room talking to me.'"

Joanne Yoho
Wauconda, Illinois
Author, *A Journey to Begin*

8.1 — INTRODUCTION

McDougal & Associates is a whole new type of Christian publishing company. You might ask, "Why do we need a new way to publish Christian books?" To us, the answer is simple:

Traditional Christian book publishing has favored a very few individual authors, choosing to publish those who were a "safe" bet financially, while ignoring the voice of the great majority of men and women called of God to speak a word to their generation. Pastors of large and wealthy congregations have sometimes found a voice through Christian self-publishers or co-publishers, but some of the most important voices of our time, the voices of the emerging prophets and priests of the hour, have all but remained silent to the Body of Christ worldwide. It's time that they are published.

Traditional Christian publishers never publish those they consider to be economically "risky," and emerging ministries often cannot afford the high cost of traditional Christian self-publishing.

The result is that the world has been robbed of an important element of the message God is speaking today. Although thousands of new books are being published each year, if your voice has not been heard, God's message to the world is incomplete. It's time for you to be heard.

A CHANGING INDUSTRY

There is another powerful reason for a new kind of publishing. We are living in the twenty-first century, technology has changed dramatically, and we must use all that God has placed at our disposal. Why settle for traditional Christian publishing when you can have your message published in book form and in the latest and most popular digital formats quickly and economically? It's your time to be heard, and we're ready to help you fulfill that mandate. We are McDougal & Associates, your on-demand Christian book publisher.

8.2 — WHAT IS ON-DEMAND PUBLISHING?

Although this subject was covered in detail earlier in the book, here is a brief summary:

WHAT WE MEAN BY ON-DEMAND PUBLISHING

The POD (or Print-on-Demand) System is simple. Today's technology allows us to order any number of your books at one time — even a single book, if that's all you need at the moment — and those books will usually be shipped within 48 hours of the order. The amazing thing about all of this is:

☐ The cost of digital book printing is not prohibitive, as it was before.

☐ The quality of digital book printing is excellent, rivaling books done on any other printing system.

These are just two of the reasons we call this new technology REVOLUTIONARY! It's one of the true marvels of the twenty-first century, and now we can use it for the Gospel and for getting your message out.

The Benefits of Doing Your Book through an On-Demand System

There are many benefits to using this system:

- ☐ **It's quick:** Your books can usually ship within 48 hours of us placing the order.

- ☐ **There's no inventory to store:** Now you order only what you need for the immediate future because you can order more at any time, and there's therefore no need to keep more on hand than you can actually use. No more stuffed storage spaces.

- ☐ **It's less expensive:** Although small quantities of on-demand copies of a book typically cost about twice what you would spend per copy if you printed several thousand at a time, if you can't use several thousand copies, ordering that many is just wasteful. In the end, therefore, using the POD system comes out costing you less.

☐ **Your expenses are spaced out more:** Because you order only what you can use in the immediate future and then order more as you need them, your total expenses are spread out over a much longer period of time.

☐ **You can avoid packing and shipping:** Instead of packing and shipping your books to a given location for some special event, let us order them directly from our printing partner, and let the printer send them directly to the location where they will be needed.

☐ **You get distribution:** Once your book is in the POD system, it automatically becomes available on Amazon.com, BarnesandNoble.com and through major Christian distributors — Ingram Books and Baker & Taylor — to bookstores everywhere. When anyone orders a book, it is billed, then produced and shipped to them (without you doing anything at all). At the end of each month, all sales are reported to us, and at the end of 90 days, payment is received. We report sales and disburse payments to our authors quarterly. The amount each author receives is the difference between the wholesale price of the book and the production cost for that particular copy, minus 10% publisher's surcharge. There is no guarantee that your book will sell, but at the very least this gets it out there to the general public. [1]

☐ **Revisions are easy:** Your book can be easily revised at any time: Because the process is all digital, the files needed to print your book can be easily revised and updated at any time. This is a major consideration for many. [2]

THE COSTS INVOLVED IN DOING ON-DEMAND PUBLISHING

The costs of getting your book into this system are surprisingly small:

☐ There is a one-time printer setup fee of just $100.00.

☐ If a physical proof is required, there is a fee of $30 (including overnight shipping). Most proofing is now done

---

1. The printer charges a $12 per year marketing access fee that makes this possible.
2. The printer charges a fee of $40 for each revision, and hourly rates may apply to text and cover changes and the reprocessing of files.

online, however, so this is not absolutely required.

☐ After that, your charges will be per copy for the number of books you order. This can vary from $1.54 per copy and up, depending on the size of your book, plus shipping and a 10% publisher's surcharge. Email us for specific quotes.

If you can use 1,500 or more copies of your book at one time, we can do it by offset and save money, still keeping the title within the POD distribution system. When 2,500 or more copies are ordered at one time, the digital price per copy now outstrips the offset price. Let us give you a quote today.

Our POD partner is Lighting Source International, with presses in the U.S., the U.K., and Australia.

8.3 — What Is McDougal & Associates?

McDougal & Associates was formed in 2004 to help spread the Gospel of Jesus Christ to as many people as possible in the shortest time possible because studies have shown that this can be done most effectively by utilizing the printed word (and now eBooks). We are blessed today to be living in the twenty-first century and have at our disposal a technological breakthrough in publishing that makes it possible to publish a book quickly and easily and to order as many or as few copies of that book as necessary at any given time. At McDougal & Associates, you may order 50 copies of your book, or you may order 50,000, and reordering any number of copies in the future is just as easy.

McDougal & Associates is made up of a group of dedicated servants of the Lord burdened for the Lord's will in the earth and eager to see His true servants heard everywhere. Our motive is never money, but His voice. We invite you to compare our prices even with other

Christian web publishers. You'll be pleasantly surprised to find that no one can beat the prices we offer. For instance, we mark up the cost of printing only 10%. When authors want copies of their book, we partner with on-demand printers here in the U.S. and in several other countries, and what they charge us is passed on, with only a 10% surcharge. In short, McDougal & Associates is here to serve you.

Harold and Andrea "Andy" McDougal are the McDougals behind McDougal & Associates. Harold has been working directly in Christian publishing now for nearly thirty-five years, and during that time, has written, ghost written, edited, and/or published more than seven hundred books. He wrote his first book in 1965, more than fifty years ago.

Aside from working on his own books on an ongoing basis, Harold has had a burden to get other ministries published and has helped dozens of them to achieve this goal. Among the best known were Ruth Ward Heflin, William A. Ward, Judson Cornwall, Les Brown, Wade Taylor, Charlotte Baker, Cal Pierce, Sandy Kirk, Jamie Lash, and Tim Bagwell. He has done many projects for other publishers including books for Dennis Leonard, Darryl Brister, Charles Blake, Darlene Bishop, and many other well known Christian leaders here in the US and abroad.

The "Associates" in McDougal & Associates are men and women of every race and of many nationalities who have a *rhema* word from God for our time and have chosen this venue as a means of having their message heard. You may choose to become an associate by choosing to publish your book/s with us.

8.4 — WHAT IS MY ROLE IN ALL OF THIS?

Our website asks the following questions:

- ☐ Are you looking for a suitable editor, one who will handle your materials with the respect and spiritual insight they deserve?

- ☐ Are you tired of pompous production managers who chop your material to pieces and destroy or change the essence of its message?

- ☐ Are you tired of your materials in print not sounding like you at all and not having any of their original power?

It concludes with these words: "If you answered yes to any of these questions, then here's the answer you've been looking for!" The reason we ask these questions is that editors, even Christian editors, are famous for disrespecting the message of authors and making a book say what they or their bosses want it to say, not necessarily what the author intended. This has turned off many authors to Christian publishing altogether.

As a missionary, I experienced the work of language interpreters in many countries. Their work is a difficult one. It is not their message they are conveying, and yet they must convey it in the most effective way. My experience was that a good interpreter could actually improve the impact of my message, but a bad one could be a drag on what I was trying to say and do.

Some years later, as an editor, I discovered that I had a gift of catching the style of the author and if I had to add a transitional word or phrase here and there, the author was pleased with it. One well known African preacher, Kingsley Fletcher, said to me with amazement, "You're more African than I am." That was the greatest compliment I could have imagined, and it was typical of what other authors say.

Our site goes on to say:

"Dr. Harold McDougal has a unique set of quali-fications as an editor. He is able to combine a wide range of ministry experience with an awesome gift from God that enables him to handle prophetic teachings with the care they so richly deserve.

Through the years, he has helped such noted authors as Charlotte Baker, Judson Cornwall, Ruth Heflin, William A. Ward, Tim Bagwell, and others get their message out. More recently, he has helped Darlene Bishop of Ohio, Dr. Yvonne Capehart of Pensacola, Bishop Paul Morton of New Orleans, Bishop Dennis Leonard formerly of Denver, Bishop Daryl Brister of Houston, Bishop Charles Blake of Los Angeles and many others. In all, he has worked on more than 700 manuscripts.

"As an editor, writer and ghostwriter, Harold has done work for Destiny Image Publishers of Shippensburg, Pennsylvania, McDougal Publishing of Hagerstown, Maryland, Whitaker House of Pittsburgh, Pennsylvania, Legacy Publishers International of Denver, Colorado, and Maxgan Associates of Rice, Virginia."

On the following pages, see what some of our published authors have had to say about McDougal & Associates and our editorial and publishing services.

"Thank God for the giftings He has invested in His people. I wish to thank Harold McDougal personally for taking this book and making it say what it needed to say. Thanks, Harold, for becoming an extended hand to hear my heart and finish off this work — getting it ready for people out there everywhere. Your calm way of approaching the work is inspirational."

Andre van Zyl ,
Good News to the Nations, Dacula, Georgia
Author, *Feed the Camels*
and *Finally, God Makes Sense*

"I personally believe that every appointment we have in life is a divine appointment, and that describes my friendship and working relationship with Dr. Harold McDougal. When the Lord commissioned me to write a book, I was willing to step out in faith and obey, but I didn't know where to begin. The Lord, however, is faithful, and He directed my footsteps in this walk of faith, introducing me to this mighty man who became my publisher.

"From the beginning, we had a strong spiritual connection, and that allowed the desired creativity to flow. I could never have imagined that what had begun as a series of teachings for my congregation would eventually turn into a powerful printed book, but that's what this man made happen for me. The book he produced was written and then printed with a spirit of excellence, and I am very grateful and pleased with the level of quality at every turn.

"Brother Harold always goes the extra mile in everything he does, and he certainly went above and beyond what was expected to aid me through this journey. He made himself available, time after time, to answer any question we had regarding the whole process, and he provided us with an enormous amount of information that enabled us to understand every step of the way.

"Personally, I appreciate Brother Harold's integrity and the joy he demonstrates in his work. This *is just my first book, and we intend to work with McDougal & Associates on at least two more sequels. God is so good!"*

David Jones
Little David Ministries,
Charlotte, North Carolina
Author, *Humble is the Way*
and *They Thought They Had Time*

"Dear Brother McDougal,

"I wish to take this opportunity to thank you for the outstanding job you did in bringing my book to completion. I was quite pleased with the outcome, the book is doing well, has been very well received and the direction is all positive. None of this would have been so without your efforts. I am looking forward to engaging you on my next book project. Thanks again."

Donald Gandy
Rice, Virginia
Author, *A Tablespoon of Love, A Tablespoon of Disciple: The Recipe for Raising a Child*

"Several years ago now, while I was traveling with Evangelist Bob Shattles, he said to me one day, 'Eddie, when you get ready to write a book, you have to get Harold McDougal to do it for you,' and he went on to tell me what an encouragement Harold had been to him. Later, I not only met Harold, but we shared a lunch together, along with our dear friend, the late Ruth Ward Heflin. I never forgot that lunch, or the kind, gentle spirit that God has so delicately adorned Harold McDougal with. I left the restaurant that day in Ashland, Virginia, knowing that I had met more than a publisher; I had a friend.

"Now these many years later, I know why Bob Shattles' enthusiasm for me to seek Harold to do my publishing was so important. I was not disappointed with my books, my relationship with McDougal & Associates or the professional and affordable manner in which the books were produced. If you choose McDougal & Associates, when your book publishing experience is over, you'll have more than a superb, top quality printing; you'll have a friend for life!"

Eddie T. Rogers
Revival In Power, Bremen, Georgia
Author, *The Power of Impartation*
and *Supernatural*

"I would like to express my gratitude for all your hard work, your insight and the professional manner you exhibited in the preparation and publication of my book. You made this journey very easy for me. I felt great joy and expectation rise up within me as I saw my words, thoughts and expressions brought to life on the pages before me. And then the person you selected to design the cover brought it to life on the outside as you continued to help me bring it to life on the inside. I'm sure that in the days to come many will be healed and blessed because you took the time to help someone who knew so little about writing a book. Thank you again."

Jody Amato
Pastor, Highway to Heaven,
Walker, Louisiana
Author, *Cinderella's Slipper*
and *If the Shoe Fits*

"Brother McDougal,

"I want to thank you for helping me get my books published. It seems obvious to me that you are anointed for this type of work. With my many questions, you have taken the time to successfully answer them all.

"You certainly read my heart as you were editing my manuscript. I am very pleased at how it turned out. What a tremendous part you play as you intertwine with ministries around the world as they strive to keep the message of the Gospel going forward.

"It has been a pleasure to work with you. I would certainly recommend you to others and plan to use you again in the future. May the Lord richly bless you and give you much favor."

Mary Cummings
Shekinah Ministries
Shreveport, Louisiana
Author, *The Restlessness of the Call*
and *People of the Presence*

"I wholeheartedly thank McDougal & Associates and Harold McDougal for the guidance and expertise that was provided with publishing my book. It was a project that involved heartfelt prayer, in order to reflect our heavenly Father's desire to spark the Body of Christ with a desire for soulwinning. Brother McDougal was able to transform vision and inspired writing into a devotional style workbook that is guaranteed to equip Christians to reach out to the world around them.

"I believe that the book was edited with a true motivation to maintain the heart of the book as it was originally written. Suggestions on layout and formatting helped transform it into a format that would promote ease for reading and understanding, whether the book is used by individuals, in Bible studies or by entire churches. With each step of the publication process, integrity and excellence were two key factors that were maintained.

"As a new Christian author, I was given the time and guidance that cannot always be experienced with other publishing companies. I think what mattered to me most about McDougal & Associates is their stated vision 'to spread the Gospel of the Lord Jesus Christ to as many people as possible in the shortest time possible.' They co-

labored with me to develop a valuable written tool to equip Christians to further the Kingdom of God by stepping out in faith and winning souls."
Susan C. Skelley
Daytona Beach Shores, Florida
Author, *Awakening to the Heartbeat of God*

"Commendation for Harold McDougal and Mc-Dougal & Associates:

"To a first-time Christian author, the idea of finding a suitable editor/publisher can raise anxiety in the heart of the strongest. This is at least how I felt as I came to the realization that there was much about the literary world that I did not understand and that, if I wanted my work to be readable and read, that it would have to be reorganized, rewritten, and reborn.

"With some trembling I approached an author friend for counsel. After all she had published her first title, which I enjoyed reading, and was working on a sequel. Without hesitation, she recommended Harold McDougal as the man to seek out. And I did that.

"My fears before our first encounter were these:

- That the editor would rip up my work, destroying the spiritual themes, making them secular or worse, carnal.
- That the rewrite would lose the essence of my passion and fail to get 'my' messages across.
- That once the content was ripped, I would have no recourse but to go with the changes.
- That the project would cost more than I could afford and more than the service was worth.

"I could not have been more wrong on each count. My experience has been more than I could have hoped for. Harold is not only a literary professional but also a sensitive and spiritual Christian. It took explanation on explanation, but he was relentless in capturing the heart of my writing and making it enjoyable and edifying to read.

"I consider Harold McDougal to be not only a professional helper and mentor, but a true brother in the Body of Christ."

Thomas W. James
Tree of Life Ministries
Statesville, North Carolina
Author, *Be Reconciled!*

"I have the pleasure of recommending Brother Harold McDougal and McDougal & Associates as a fine Christian publishing company. I was very fortunate to have such a man of God, as well as a seasoned publisher of his caliber, to work with me in the preparation and publishing of my book. Harold has a heart to help anyone who is engaged in spreading the Gospel of Jesus Christ. His work exceeded my greatest expectations, and his expertise not only blessed me. It now blesses everyone who reads the book.

"It was amazing how he was able to capture my heart, my life and what God has given to me and express it in the pages of the book. And the resulting message is clear and concise.

"At a more personal level, Harold is a well-disciplined, industrious man with a pleasant personality. He went beyond my requirements in the quality of the work he rendered. Not only were his services of the highest quality; his prices were also reasonable. I highly recommend this ministry to all of my friends."

Lee Edward Gaddie
New Jerusalem Whole Truth Church, Humble, Texas
Author, *The Commander's Anointing*

"I would like to recommend my publisher, Brother Harold McDougal, as a man of integrity. He is one of the kindest persons I know. When I started to write my book, Growing in the Glory, *he and his wife had the most encouraging words to help me with the project I have know him now for more than twenty years, when I was just starting out in ministry. As an author, his books helped to build my faith and the foundation of God's Word in my life. Now God has used his talents to catapult me forward into my destiny. I will always be grateful for my association with McDougal & Associates. May God continue to use the influence of this great company to bless other upcoming authors, so that they, too, can fulfill their vision in His Kingdom."*

Carol Hylton,
Brooklyn, New York
Missionary and English Pastor
El Shaddai Haitian Church of God
Author, *Growing in the Glory*

"Harold made the process of transitioning to published Christian writing so easy for me. He was helpful at every step. His knowledge of the Scriptures was invaluable. I had no former knowledge of the world of professional publishing, and so everything was new. Harold made it easy. He patiently explained each step and the myriad of details. Then he let me respond at my own pace, so that I was not overwhelmed. We have published three books so far with him and expect another one down the road. I highly recommend McDougal & Associates to anyone who wants to get God's Word out to the world."

Donald C. Mann
Landenberg, Pennsylvania
Author, *Discovering Our Redemption,*
Battle Prayer for Divine Healing
and *OK, God, Now What?*

"I have been highly recommending McDougal & Associates to family and friends, and I will continue to do so. People are buying the book. The title and cover design catch their attention immediately, and then, when they open the book and see the layout, they love it. Thank you for that. There are other books that I must write, so you have not seen the last of me. To be continued. God Bless You."

Linda Gourdine-Hunt
Divine Inspirations Messenger
Author, *Help Wanted!*
and
Good Evening, Heavenly Father. How Was Your Day?

"Harold,

I'm so pleased that God led me to your publishing company. You did more than publish a book. You critiqued, edited, and helped in every way possible with the patience of Job. God bless you in this unique ministry He has given you."

Lowell Lytle
Captain of the Titanic
Pinellas Park, Florida
Author, *Diving into the Deep*

"As a first-time writer I was incredibly nervous about finding a publisher and I cried out to God that He would lead me to someone whom I could trust and feel safe with. He answered my prayers by leading me to Harold McDougal. From the start Harold treated me with respect and kindness, despite my being so new in the whole writing process. I was thoroughly blessed by his wonderful combination of professionalism, integrity and sensitivity to the Holy Spirit. I would warmly recommend him as a seasoned and gifted publisher and see it is an as honor that I was able to work together with him on my book."

Amanda Goransson
Gothenburg, Sweden
Author, *Warrior Women Arise*

"I am writing to let you know how much I appreciate the outstanding service you provided. I was inexperienced in this area, but you made it so easy and a lot less stressful than I imagined. You were very attentive and helpful. You interacted with me throughout the process and that was very encouraging. You are very knowledgeable and professional and seemed genuinely interested in helping me accomplish this Kingdom assignment.

"Because of your efforts, I am able to get my message out to the world, and I am very satisfied with choosing you as my publisher. I will continue to use your services in the future, as well as recommend it to others. I thank God for you and pray His continued blessing over your business. I look forward to working with your again in the future."

Pastor R. W. Kendrick
Baton Rouge, Louisiana
Author, *Lord, Help Me! I'm "Failing" in Love!*

Book Sizes, Paper Selection, Bindings and Font Selection

Book Sizes

Although we can do many different book sizes, we specialize in the following popular trade sizes:

4.37 X 7
5 X 8
5.5 X 8.5
6 X 9

Paper Selection

Unless printing a book in full color, we are limited to two paper selections:

White 50 lb
Créme 50 lb

Bindings

Our most popular binding is perfect bound, but we can also do saddle stitch, case laminate, and hardback with or without dust jacket.

Font Selection

We have a wide variety of fonts to choose from. Email us for samples of our most popular book fonts.

Dear Reader,

I know that I have given you a lot of material to digest. I recommend that you come back, from time to time, and review it. Each time you do, you will be reaching new levels of understanding in your own publishing ministry, new thoughts will be quickened to you and your own creative energies will be ignited.

My prayer is that these suggestions will help you in your publishing venture and will make it both financially and spiritually rewarding. If we can assist you in the publication and promotion of your book, please don't hesitate to call on us. We want to help you to be a blessing to all those around you.

Harold McDougal

Infallible Proofs

Rediscovering the Christ Amidst the Clutter of our Twenty-First Century World

Harold McDougal

I Can Do This

Overcoming Life's Seemingly Impossible Situations

Harold McDougal

Understanding
the
SEED

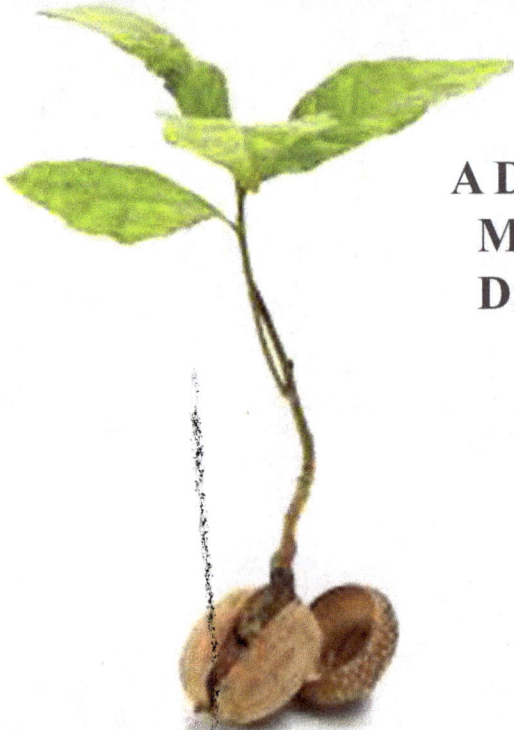

**A Divine Road
Map for the
Days Ahead**

Peter Kange
Jane Lowder
Harold McDougal
and

Andrea "Andy" McDougal

McDougal & Associates
Your Print-On-Demand Publisher
18896 Greenwell Springs Road
Greenwell Spring, LA 70739

225-262-1937

www.ThePublishedWord.com

HaroldM@ThePublishedWord.com

www.ingramcontent.com/pod-product-compliance
Lightning Source LLC
Chambersburg PA
CBHW070032100426
42740CB00013B/2672